# BEYOND THE BINARY

## Publications of the Boston Psychoanalytic Society and Institute Library

*Beyond the Binary: Essays on Gender* is the fourth publication sponsored by the Library Committee of the Boston Psychoanalytic Society and Institute. Previous works include:

*Edward Bibring Photographs the Psychoanalysts of his Time, 1932–1938* (2005), published in conjunction with Psychosozial-Verlag (German and English editions). These rare photographs, first discovered in the BPSI archives by librarian and photographer Vivien Goldman, capture intimate (and never before reproduced) images of psychoanalytic pioneers at meetings of the International Psychoanalytical Association.

*Freud and Me* (2006) is a collection of reflections by several faculty members and candidates of BPSI on their relation to Freud and his work, in commemoration of Freud's 150th birthday.

*Grete Bibring: A Culinary Biography* (2015) tells the story of Grete's life in Vienna, London, and Boston. Her notebooks (found in our archives), spanning forty years, list her guests at her dinner parties and what she served. They indicate her continued sense of order in a life disrupted by war, emigration, change of language, and psychoanalytic power struggles.

# BEYOND THE BINARY

## Essays on Gender

*Edited by*
### Shari Thurer

Published with the help of the members of the Library Committee
Boston Psychoanalytic Society and Institute

*James Barron, PhD*
*Ellen Goldberg, PhD*
*Daniel Jacobs, MD, Director of the Library, Contributing Author*
*Delia Kostner, PhD*
*Malkah T. Notman, MD, Contributing Author*
*Marcia Smith-Hutton, LICSW, BCD*
*Rita Teusch, PhD, Contributing Author*
*Shari Thurer, ScD , Contributing Author*
*Olga Umansky, MLIS, Librarian/Archivist, Publication Assistant*
*Steven Varga-Golovcsenko, MD*

PHOENIX
PUBLISHING HOUSE
*firing the mind*

First published in 2023 by
Phoenix Publishing House Ltd
62 Bucknell Road
Bicester
Oxfordshire OX26 2DS

Published with the support of the American Psychoanalytic Foundation

British Library Cataloguing in Publication Data

A C.I.P. for this book is available from the British Library

ISBN-13: 978-1-912691-87-6

Typeset by Medlar Publishing Solutions Pvt Ltd, India

www.firingthemind.com

*For Olga Umansky*
*Librarian of the Hanns Sachs Library*
*Boston Psychoanalytic Society and Institute*
*2005–2022*

*Wise, patient, always kind*
*Without her help, this book would never have been completed*
*We wish her well.*

# Contents

# About the editor and contributors

**Robin Ely, PhD**, is the Diane Doerge Wilson Professor of Business Administration at Harvard Business School, where she conducts research on race and gender relations in organizations, with a focus on organizational culture change aimed at reducing workplace inequality. Her work is published in academic journals such as *Administrative Science Quarterly, Academy of Management Journal*, and *Academy of Management Review*, and, for practitioners, in *Harvard Business Review*. She lives most of the time in Essex, MA, in a house she built with her late husband, Harry Spence, overlooking the saltmarsh and the back of Crane Beach.

**Francesca Ely-Spence** went to Barnard College in New York City and studied sociology and women's, gender, and sexuality studies. They currently live in Boston with their rescue pup, Lucy. When not working at a local French bakery, they love to go on hikes, cook, and listen to D&D podcasts.

**Oren Gozlan, C.Psych, ABPP, FIPA**, is a psychoanalyst in private practice. He is the Chair of the Scientific Committee, and Faculty at the Toronto Institute of Psychoanalysis, the Toronto Institute of Contemporary Psychoanalysis, and the Canadian Institute for Child and Adolescent Psychoanalytic Psychotherapy. He is a member of the IPA committee for Gender Diversity and Sexuality. His book *Transsexuality and the Art of Transitioning: A Lacanian Approach* won the American Academy and Board of Psychoanalysis annual book prize for books published in 2015. He is also the winner of the Symonds Prize for 2016 and the Ralph Roughton Award for 2022. His edited collection titled *Critical Debates in the Transsexual Studies Field: In Transition* (Routledge) was a runner-up for the 2019 Gradiva Award.

**Robin Haas, LICSW**, (they/them/theirs) is a nonbinary clinical social worker and certified Life and Emotional Intelligence Coach living and working in private practice in the Boston area. Robin has dedicated their life to becoming happy and helps others do the same by recognizing their full potential. Robin helps people change their narrative so they can free themselves from self-imposed limitations. In addition to doing clinical work, Robin is a speaker and trainer with SpeakOUT Boston. They earned a degree in elementary education from Boston University and an MSW at Simmons School of Social Work.

**Daniel Jacobs, MD**, is a training and supervising analyst at the Boston Psychoanalytic Society and Institute, Faculty, and Director of the Hanns Sachs Library and Archives. Among his many publications are *The Distance from Home: A Novel* (2019), *Grete Bibring: A Culinary Biography* (2015), *Edward Bibring Photographs the*

*Psychoanalysts of his Time 1932–1938* (2005), and *The Supervisory Encounter: A Guide for Teachers of Psychodynamic Psychotherapy and Psychoanalysis* (1995).

**Malkah T. Notman, MD**, was on staff and faculty at Beth Israel Hospital, and did her residency at Boston State Hospital and Beth Israel. She participated in Bibring's pregnancy study and wrote extensively on women's reproductive issues, menopause, women's health, development and careers. A training analyst for many years, she trained and taught at Boston Psychoanalytic Society and Institute, and became its president in 1998–2001. An active faculty and Clinical Professor of Psychiatry at Harvard Medical School, Dr. Notman was also an Acting Chair of the Department of Psychiatry at Cambridge Health Alliance for four years.

**Lewis Harwood "Harry" Spence, JD** (1946–2021) was Boston Psychoanalytic Society and Institute board member, affiliate scholar, and Explorations in Mind instructor. Born in Schenectady, NY, Lewis Harwood Spence, known to his friends and colleagues as Harry, grew up in Cranbury, NJ. He received his AB in American history and literature from Harvard College, and graduated from Harvard Law School in 1974. He devoted his professional life to helping tens of thousands of people by turning around large-scale failing public institutions. He took on leadership positions for the Cambridge, Somerville, and Boston housing authorities, was the state-appointed Receiver who helped the City of Chelsea emerge from bankruptcy, became the first Administrator to help reform the Massachusetts Trial Court system, was tapped by the Governor to be the Commissioner of the Massachusetts Department of Social Services, was appointed to be the Deputy Chancellor for Operations for the New York City Board of Education, and served as Commissioner of the Massachusetts Education Leadership program. He was working on a book describing his experiences, and conceptualizing the complex dynamics of those large-scale organizational changes. He also had been a lecturer at the Harvard Kennedy School, and a lecturer and Professor of Practice at the Harvard Graduate School of Education, where he was among the original faculty directors of the Doctor of Education Leadership program.

**Rita Teusch, PhD**, is a training and supervising analyst at the Boston Psychoanalytic Society and Institute (BPSI). She is a lecturer in psychiatry (psychology), part time, at Harvard Medical School, Cambridge Health Alliance. She regularly teaches courses on Freud and Klein at BPSI. Her publications and book essays cover the topics of trauma, eating disorders, the history of psychoanalysis, and social justice. She has a private practice in Harvard Square, Cambridge.

**Shari Thurer, ScD**, is a Boston Psychoanalytic Society and Institute psychotherapist and Library Committee member, an Adjunct Associate Professor at Boston University, a psychologist in Boston, and the author of many noted publications, including *Myths of Motherhood: How Culture Reinvents the Good Mother* (Houghton Mifflin Harcourt, 1994) and *The End of Gender: A Psychological Autopsy* (Routledge, 2005).

# Introduction

*Rita Teusch*

In the last two decades, clinicians have witnessed a profound change with regard to gender identifications in an increasing number of our patients. Many patients are experiencing and defining their gender and sexuality in much more variable and nuanced ways besides male or female, gay or straight, and some choose to not use these labels at all. This has been especially true of younger patients, who are increasingly rejecting binary gender assignments and asking us to accept their more fluid and nuanced gender identifications. Many of these patients do not see their gender identifications as a source of conflict but rather as an expression of their authentic selves. The greater acceptance of nontraditional gender identifications has also encouraged those who have long been "in the closet" to come forward and share their experiences and suffering due to having been nonbinary all their lives.

In December 2021, the American Psychoanalytic Association (APsaA) voted to affirm their commitment to nondiscrimination against diverse identity characteristics, and the training standards for psychoanalytic candidates regarding diversity were broadened and made significantly more inclusive. A person's gender identity and/or sexual preference is henceforth understood as one identity characteristic next to the identity characteristics of age, religion, race, ethnic background, and socioeconomic and ability status.

> It is the policy of the American Psychoanalytic Association that an applicant for candidacy is never excluded or discriminated against on the basis of age, gender, sexual orientation, religious affiliation, race, ethnic background, or ability status.
>
> (APsaA, pp. 9–10)

> Candidates are expected to work with cases reflecting a diversity of identity characteristics including, but not limited to gender, sexual orientation, age, religion, race, ethnicity, culture, ability status, and socioeconomic status.
>
> (APsaA, p. 11)

These new training standards reflect APsaA's acknowledgment of the significant psychological impact of all identity characteristics on personality development. The expectation is that psychoanalysts become knowledgeable about and sensitized to how these identity characteristics are manifested in a patient and have shaped their psychological development. Furthermore, analysts need to be trained to become comfortable with exploring psychoanalytically how various identity characteristics interact to affect an individual's conscious experience and their unconscious feelings and conflicts.

At the suggestion of the Library Committee, a small group of Boston Psychoanalytic Society and Institute (BPSI) therapists and analysts, led by Shari Thurer, set out a couple of years ago to explore the history of BPSI's and the larger analytic community's changing views on homosexuality. Our discussions soon turned to the rapidly changing views on gender in society and also in our field. Defining gender by anatomical sex alone no longer describes the gender experience and sexuality for many of our patients, and gender is no longer predictable of particular psychological traits. We realized that we were again at a crucial turning point with regard to traditionally narrow, often prejudicial views on gender. We decided that it was important to increase our knowledge of and empathy with the kaleidoscope of gender identifications of fellow clinicians and patients. We believed that it was important that, as a discipline, we avoid doing harm again by being exclusionary and discriminatory and/or pathologizing those who do not fit into our traditionally narrow definition of gender.

The result of our research and writings, conducted in consultation with BPSI candidates knowledgeable in the area of gender diversity, is the following series of essays and personal reflections. We realize that this monograph explores only a limited number of gender-related topics, focusing for the most part on nonbinary gender. Clearly, there is so much more to learn about the gender revolution that is currently taking place, and this is only the beginning of a discussion.

We offer this monograph, the fourth in the BPSI Library Committee Series, as a step in the process of better understanding the lived gender experience and complex gender identifications of an increasing number of our colleagues and patients. Our goal is to open up a conversation to further explore the topic of nonbinary and other genders that is increasingly being written about in the therapy and psychoanalytic literature, often with considerable controversy. An example of current controversial views can be found in *The International Journal of Psychoanalysis, 101*(5) (2020).

We invite you to begin to talk with us together or find your own ways to educate yourself further on this important topic.

The following essays are personal reflections by interested clinicians, patients, and BPSI-affiliated academic scholars of various generations. This monograph is by no means BPSI's definitive statement on nonbinary gender. We hope that you will listen with us to the voices of those who were brave enough to share their gender-related experiences. We have found that listening carefully and with an open mind (rather than raising questions immediately) to those whose experiences with and feelings about their gender do not fit into our traditional binary assumptions is a crucial first step to bringing about acceptance and healing.

## Reference

The American Psychoanalytic Association Board of Directors (2021, December 12). Standards and Principles for Psychoanalytic Education. https://apsa.org/sites/default/files/Standards-PrinciplesForPsa-Education.pdf

# CHAPTER ONE

# Psychoanalysis meets they

*Shari Thurer*

> *We're all born naked and the rest is drag.*
>
> —RuPaul

Once there were two genders: male and female. Males typically were the big hairy ones who left the toilet seat up. Females were the less hairy ones who put the toilet seat down … It was easy to tell them apart. These days it's not so easy.

I wrote this in *The End of Gender: A Psychological Autopsy* (Thurer, 2005), in which I pointed out that the genders are leaking into each other. But instead of gender distinctions disappearing, it turns out that the categories of gender have morphed. In 2014, Facebook listed fifty-six gender options, while Facebook in the UK offered users seventy-one (Hartocollis, 2020). It also provided a custom gender choice.

Even such bastions of the establishment as Harvard's renowned Kennedy School of Government agreed, in 2020, to provide plastic stickers with four pronoun options that students could apply to their name cards: he/him, she/her, they/them, and ze/hir. In line with this proliferation of gender diversity, the toy manufacturer Mattel, betting on where it thinks the country is going, created a gender-neutral doll, outfitted with both camo pants and tutus, as well as boy bobs and long wigs, so children may mix and match gender as they wish, creating multiple possibilities, personalized chimeras. Today many young people's chosen pronoun for themselves is "they," hence the title of this essay.

So where is psychoanalytic theory regarding this mainstream surge in gender-bending? Psychoanalyst Susan Vaughan noted at the American Psychoanalytic Association's national meeting in 2020 that "trans" is the new "gay," by which I assume she means that transgender is the next in line to be considered "normal." But what about the fifty-five other nonbinary gender options? Apparently, psychoanalytic thinking is advancing, but is still behind the bell curve.

When it comes to the array of gender identities folks are embracing, the big question is whether this is just for media attention and public notice or a reflection of true variance that has long existed but went unexpressed in past generations. Perhaps young people today feel freer to convey nontraditional gender identities that were present but unacknowledged all along. Indeed, nonbinary sexual orientation (to be distinguished from gender identity) has gone from the margins to the mainstream. By some counts, there are more than 120 regular or recurring LBGTQ characters on cable TV and streaming sites (Wolfe & Ries, 2019). Perhaps gender identity may go the same way as sexual orientation. Talk to American teenagers, and they may describe themselves as pangender, a-romantic, asexual, genderqueer, two-spirit, genderless, demigirl, no gender, and on and on. Courageous or intentionally provocative, hyper-individualistic, "you-do-you" young people from across the United States are up-ending convention and saying that they aren't male or female, but perhaps neither or maybe both.

Or perhaps this variance is an illusion, a product of a category mistake—the assumption that there is such a thing as gender and that its manifestations have a common core. The Argentine writer Jorge Luis Borges satirizes the human tendency to classify things in his essay "The Analytical Language of John Wilkins," in which he whimsically refers to a fictional Chinese encyclopedia, titled *Celestial Emporium of Benevolent Knowledge*, that classified animals in fourteen categories:

> On those remote pages it is written that animals are divided into (a) those that belong to the Emperor, (b) embalmed ones, (c) those that are trained, (d) suckling pigs, (e) mermaids or sirens, (f) fabled ones, (g) stray dogs, (h) those that are included in this classification, (i) those that tremble as if they were mad, (j) innumerable ones, (k) those drawn with a very fine camel's hair brush, (l) et cetera, (m) those that have just broken a vase, (n) those that from afar look like flies.

In other words, Borges suggests that the way we categorize things is arbitrary. Perhaps, then, the way we classify gender expression is arbitrary. Unfortunately, we assign value judgments to these expressions: analyzable/unanalyzable; normal/abnormal. Psychoanalytic theory persists in this.

If the new visibility and acceptance of homosexual individuals derails our conception of ordinary gender arrangements, then the new visibility and acceptance of nonbinary gender amounts to an intellectual train wreck. Gone is the requirement that a gender identity cohere with your genitals. These days, it's not unusual to be one gender on the internet and another in bed. For some, all attributes once considered to be specific to a particular sex, including the very feeling of being male or female, are up for grabs and may yo-yo back and forth.

Gender-bending is the new beat of pop stars, Olympic athletes, cartoon characters, fashionistas, perfume makers, and young intellectuals, many of whom have taken to flaunting a self-styled potpourri of male and female characteristics—think Caitlyn Jenner, Laverne Cox, Chaz Bono, Kristen Stewart, and Emma Corrin, who recently portrayed Diana, Princess of Wales on TV's *The Crown*. They're all over cartoons and manga. Even Bugs Bunny, while definitively male, trades on crossdressing. Regarding attributes like gender role, identity, and sexual preference, and now gender identification, we're apparently more smorgasbord than *menu fixe*.

Data regarding the prevalence of folks who identify as nonbinary are limited, but the ubiquity of the subgroup of transgender individuals is not trivial. In a large survey of American high school students, 1.8% of young people identify as transgender. Interestingly, cohorts younger than eighteen to twenty-four years old identify at a sharply higher rate than those older, suggesting increased societal acceptance these days (Centers for Disease Control and Prevention, 2019). Social media like Tumblr make it easier for young people to find themselves—and each other. But sadly, transgender young people still report significantly higher rates of depression, suicidality, and victimization compared to their cisgender peers.

The nomenclature for these various identities can be confusing and is constantly evolving. A number of different glossaries are available. This especially current and comprehensive list (forthcoming, Johns Hopkins University Press) was developed by Genny Beemyn, Director of the Stonewall Center at the University of Massachusetts Amherst, and Mickey Eliason, Professor and Assistant Dean for Faculty Development/Scholarship at San Francisco State University. It encompasses the whole range of gender identity, sexual/emotional attraction, and romantic relationships. Material in brackets is mine.

**Aces or asexual people:** Individuals who generally experience little or no sexual attraction to others of any gender.

**Agender people:** Individuals who identify as not having a gender. Agender people may identify as genderless, gender-neutral, or neutrois (having an unknown or indefinable gender), or decide not to label their gender.

**AGs or aggressives:** Lesbians who express themselves in a masculine manner, such as by binding their breasts. They are also called studs. The terms are more commonly used in communities of color.

**Alloromantic people:** Individuals who experience romantic attraction to others of any gender (i.e., people who are not aromantic).

**Allosexual or zsexual people:** Individuals who experience sexual attraction to others of any gender (i.e., people who are not asexual).

**Amatonormativity:** The assumption that a central, exclusive, amorous relationship is a universally shared goal for all people and is valued over all other relationship types.

**Androgyne people:** Individuals whose gender identity is simultaneously male and female or in between male and female and whose gender expression is often androgynous, combining both traditionally feminine and masculine characteristics (although not necessarily in equal amounts).

**Androromantic people:** Individuals who experience romantic attraction toward men, males, and/or masculinity, regardless of whether the people they are attracted to were assigned male at birth.

**Androsexual people:** Individuals who experience sexual attraction toward men, males, and/or masculinity, regardless of whether the people they are attracted to were assigned male at birth.

**Aros or aromantic people:** Individuals who generally experience little or no romantic attraction to others of any gender.

**Bi or bisexual people:** Individuals who experience sexual, romantic, and/or emotional attractions to people of more than one gender.

**Bigender people:** Individuals who experience their gender identity as two genders at the same time or whose gender identity may vary between two genders.

**Binary trans people:** Individuals who identify as trans women or trans men.

**Biromantic people:** Individuals who are romantically, but not necessarily sexually, attracted to people of more than one gender.

**Bois:** Individuals assigned female at birth who identify their gender as nonbinary. Because they are not male-identified, they are "bois" and not "boys."

**Butches:** Individuals of any gender or sexual identity who present and act in traditionally masculine ways, which could include being the "dominant" partner in sexual relationships.

**Chosen name:** The name that someone uses for themselves. The term "preferred name" should not be used because the name that a trans person goes by is not a preference.

**Cis or cisgender people:** Individuals who identify with the sex that was assigned to them at birth (i.e., people who are not trans).

**Cisnormativity:** The assumption that cisgender is the default or norm and that being cis is more valued than all other gender identities, which results in the marginalization and erasure of trans and gender-nonconforming people. It is rooted in the erroneous beliefs that gender is a binary (women and men) and that sex assigned at birth is immutable.

**Crossdressers:** Individuals who present their gender in ways that are traditionally associated with people of a gender different from how they were assigned at birth *[preferred term to "transvestites"]*.

**Dead name:** The first name assigned at birth to a trans person that they do not use for themselves.

**Demigender people:** Individuals who feel a partial connection to a particular gender identity. Examples of demigender identities include demigirl, demiboy, and demiandrogyne.

**Demiromantic people:** Individuals who typically do not feel romantic attraction to someone unless they have already formed a strong emotional bond with the person.

**Demis or demisexual people:** Individuals who typically do not feel sexual attraction to someone unless they have already formed a strong emotional bond with the person.

**Dyadic people:** Individuals who are born with chromosomes, a reproductive system, and a sexual anatomy that fit into the prevailing standard for "female" or "male" individuals (i.e., people who are not intersex).

**Dyadism or binarism:** The societal, institutional, and individual beliefs and practices that assume that there are only two "biological" or "natural" sexes—female and male. Dyadism/binarism privileges dyadic people and leads to prejudice and discrimination against people with intersex variations.

**Feminine of center people:** Individuals assigned male at birth who tend toward the feminine in their gender identity/expression.

**Femmes:** Individuals of any gender or sexual identity who present and act in traditionally feminine ways, which could include being the "subordinate" partner in sexual relationships.

**Gay men:** Men who experience sexual, romantic, and/or emotional attractions to other men.

**Gender binary:** The social system that sees only two genders and that requires everyone to be raised as a man or a woman, depending on the sex assigned to them at birth.

**Gender fluid people:** Individuals whose gender varies over time. A gender fluid person may at any time identify as male, female, agender, or any other nonbinary gender identity, or as some combination of gender identities.

**Gender-inclusive or gender-expansive facilities:** Bathrooms, restrooms, and locker rooms that are open to people of all genders. They may be single- or multiple-user facilities.

**Gender-inclusive or gender-expansive housing:** Residence hall rooms that are assigned regardless of gender, so that a student can have a roommate(s) of any gender. Sometimes "gender-neutral housing" is used, but this term is increasingly seen as inappropriate because it implies that the concept of gender is being neutralized or erased, rather than being expanded and embraced.

**Genderism:** The societal, institutional, and individual beliefs and practices that assume that there are only two genders and that gender is determined by one's sex assignment at birth or by specific sex characteristics. Genderism privileges cis people and leads to prejudice and discrimination against trans and gender-nonconforming people.

**Gender-nonconforming people:** Individuals who do not adhere to the traditional gender expectations for appearance and behavior of people of their assigned sex. Some identify as trans, but others do not.

**Genderqueer people:** Individuals who identify as neither male nor female (but as another gender), as somewhere in between or beyond genders, or as a combination of genders.

**Graces, gray A's, or gray asexuals:** Individuals whose sexual attraction exists within the gray area between sexual and asexual. They experience sexual attraction infrequently or not very strongly. Other terms that are used to describe this identity are semisexual, asexual-ish, and sexual-ish.

**Gray romantics:** Individuals whose romantic attraction exists within the gray area between romantic and aromantic. They experience romantic attraction infrequently or not very strongly.

**Gynoromantic people:** Individuals who experience romantic attraction toward women, females, and/or femininity, regardless of whether the people they are attracted to were assigned female at birth.

**Gynosexual/gynesexual people:** Individuals who experience sexual attraction toward women, females, and/or femininity, regardless of whether the people they are attracted to were assigned female at birth.

**Heteroflexible people:** Individuals who are primarily attracted to people of a gender different from themselves and who typically identify as heterosexual, but who may engage in same-sex sexual activity in certain situations. As it is defined by the Urban Dictionary, "I'm straight but shit happens."

**Heteronormativity:** The assumption that heterosexuality is the default or norm and that being heterosexual is more valued than all other sexual identities, which results in the marginalization and erasure of LGBQ+ people.

**Heteroromantic people:** Individuals who are romantically, but not necessarily sexually, attracted to people of a gender different from themselves.

**Heterosexism:** The societal, institutional, and individual beliefs and practices that assume that all people are heterosexual. Heterosexism privileges heterosexual people and leads to prejudice and discrimination against asexual, lesbian, gay, bisexual, pansexual, and other people with non-heterosexual sexual identities.

**Heterosexual or straight people:** Men who experience sexual, romantic, and/or emotional attractions to women, and women who experience sexual, romantic, and/or emotional attractions to men.

**Homoflexible people:** Individuals who are primarily attracted to people of the same gender as themselves and who typically identify as lesbian or gay, but who may engage in sexual activity with people of a gender different from themselves in certain situations.

**Homoromantic people:** Individuals who are romantically, but not necessarily sexually, attracted to people of a gender similar to themselves.

**Intersex:** An umbrella term used to describe a wide range of natural biological variations of individuals who are born with a chromosomal pattern, a reproductive system, and/or sexual anatomy that does not fit typical binary notions of male or female bodies *[preferred term to "hermaphrodite"]*.

**Lesbians:** Women who experience sexual, romantic, and/or emotional attractions to other women.

**Lithosexual or akoisexual people:** Individuals who feel sexual attraction toward others, but do not desire reciprocation of that attraction or do not wish to enter a sexual relationship.

**Lithromantic or akoiromantic people:** Individuals who feel romantic attraction toward others, but do not desire reciprocation of that attraction or do not wish to enter a romantic relationship.

**Masculine of center people:** Individuals assigned female at birth who tend toward the masculine in their gender identity/expression.

**Monosexism:** The societal, institutional, and individual beliefs and practices that assume that all people are attracted to only one other sex or gender—that one is either exclusively heterosexual or exclusively lesbian/gay. Monosexism privileges people with binary sexual identities and leads to prejudice and discrimination against bisexual, pansexual, queer, and other people with nonbinary sexual identities.

**Neutrois people:** Individuals who identify their gender as neutral or null. They may also identify as agender.

**Nonbinary trans people:** An umbrella term for individuals who do not fit into traditional "male" and "female" gender categories. Nonbinary people include individuals who identify as agender, bigender, gender fluid, genderqueer, pangender, and many additional genders.

**Pangender people:** Individuals whose gender identity is numerous, either fixed (many at once) or fluid (moving from one gender to other genders).

**Panromantic people:** Individuals who are romantically, but not necessarily sexually, attracted to others regardless of their gender identity or biological sex.

**Pansexual or omnisexual people:** Individuals who experience sexual, romantic, and/or emotional attractions to other people regardless of their gender identity or biological sex.

**Personal pronouns:** The pronouns that someone uses for themselves. The term "preferred pronouns" should not be used because someone's pronouns are not a preference.

**Plurisexual people:** An umbrella term for individuals, including bisexual, pansexual, and polysexual individuals, who are attracted to people of more than one gender.

**Polysexual people:** Individuals who experience sexual, romantic, and/or emotional attractions to people of more than one gender and/or form of gender expression, but not to all.

**QTPOC (pronounced "cutie poc"):** Queer and trans people of color.

**Queer:** An umbrella term to refer to all LGBTQ+ people. It is also a specific identity of individuals whose sexuality and/or gender is fluid or does not fit into established categories.

**Queerplatonic:** Non-romantic relationships that involve close emotional connections that are often deeper or more intense than what is traditionally found in friendships.

**Questioning people:** Individuals who are uncertain about how they identify their gender and/or sexuality.

**Same-gender loving people:** Individuals who experience same-gender attraction. The term originated within communities of color as an alternative to "lesbian" and "gay," which they felt did not speak to their cultural heritages.

**Sapiosexual people:** Individuals who are attracted to people based on intelligence, rather than gender identity or biological sex.

**Sex assigned at birth:** Sex designation given at birth, typically based on one's genitals. Most people are assigned female at birth (AFAB) or assigned male at birth (AMAB).

**Sexually fluid people:** Individuals whose sexuality varies over time. A sexually fluid person may at any time identify as heterosexual, lesbian/gay, bisexual, or any other nonbinary sexual identity, or as some combination of sexual identities.

**Skoliosexual people:** Individuals who experience sexual, romantic, and/or emotional attractions to people with nonbinary gender identities.

**Studs:** Lesbians who express themselves in a masculine manner, such as by binding their breasts. They are also called AGs or aggressives. The term is more commonly used in communities of color.

**Third gender people:** Individuals who identify as neither male nor female but as another gender.

**Trans or transgender people:** An umbrella term for individuals whose gender identity and/or expression is different from the sex assigned to them at birth. Among individuals who might identify as transgender are binary trans people (trans women and trans men) and nonbinary trans people (individuals who identify as agender, androgyne, demigender, gender fluid, genderqueer, and other identities that go beyond traditional gender categories).

**Trans men:** Men who were assigned female at birth.

**Transmisogyny:** A term coined by trans writer and activist Julia Serano to describe the unique discrimination experienced by trans women and trans feminine individuals, who face a combination of anti-trans and anti-women beliefs and practices.

**Trans women:** Women who were assigned male at birth.

**Two-spirit people:** A pan-Indian term for individuals in traditional Indigenous cultures in North America who identified and were recognized as neither female nor male. The term is also used by some contemporary LGBTQ+ Indigenous people to describe themselves *[preferred term to "berdache"]*.

The list does not include the term "gender dysphoria," defined in the American Psychiatric Association's *Diagnostic and Statistical*

*Manual of Mental Disorders: DSM* (2013) as "a marked incongruence between one's experienced/expressed gender and assigned gender." Most people who experience this "incongruence" strongly object to being listed in the DSM, arguing that it serves to dehumanize and pathologize them.

This list also does not address the topic of gender-affirming surgery, surgical procedures that change one's body to conform to one's gender identity. These procedures may include "top surgery" (breast augmentation or removal) and "bottom surgery" (altering genitals). For female-to-male transsexual individuals, surgeries involve a bilateral mastectomy (chest reconstruction) and/or oophorectomy/panhysterectomy (removal of the ovaries, uterus, and cervix), and sometimes a phalloplasty (construction of a penis) and scrotoplasty (formation of a scrotum) or a metoidioplasty (restructuring the clitoris). For male-to-female transsexual individuals, surgeries consist of optional surgical breast implants and vaginoplasty (construction of a vagina). Additional surgeries might include a trachea shave (reducing the size of the Adam's apple), bone restructuring to feminize facial features, and hair transplants. Gender-affirming surgery is sometimes referred to as "gender reassignment surgery" or "gender-confirming surgery."

The trajectory of the term "queer" mirrors the trajectory of acceptance of nonbinary gender. Formerly pejorative, meaning "strange" or "peculiar," it is now an umbrella term for all LGBTQ+ people. In the late 1980s, however, the term was a political hot potato used by activists as a radical alternative to more assimilationist branches of the LGBT community. But by the 1990s, the term "queer" was reclaimed by cooler, more level-headed cohorts. It was used to label the theory—queer theory—that challenged the idea that gender is a manifestation of one's core, natural self, and claimed, instead, that it is socially constructed. In other words, the meaning placed on gender is invented. It would not exist had people not built it, and we need not have built it at all, at least not in its present form.

What queer theorists argue, with their tongues resolutely out of their cheeks, is that there is no such thing as gender difference because there is no such thing as gender. They contend that dividing people up into two groups based on the shape of their genitals is but a cultural invention, and a poor one, for it creates a false dichotomy. Such a division is too crude, linear, tunnel-visioned, coercive. The gender binary, according to queer theory, is not writ in the stars, the primordial soup, the collective unconscious, or our genes. It was created by a privileged class, the demographically dominant, those people whose numbers and status entitled them to define the world according to their own blueprints (in Western culture: straight, white men). Put differently, those in power get to assign meaning. So, our particular idea about what constitutes gender is just that: an idea, not an eternal verity. Our predecessors followed a different pattern from our own, and our descendants may hew to one that is no less different. Hence the propensity for young people to refer to themselves and each other as "they" so as not to anchor their bodies to the pronouns "he" or "she." This is one of the major tenets of queer theory.

Starting in the 1990s, queer theory, aka postmodern gender theory, spawned a cottage industry in dense texts. Interestingly, most of these were written by academics in philosophy or literary studies, not clinicians. Simply put, queer theory is about trying to understand different kinds of gender identification and desire and how culture defines and judges them. It holds that individual sexuality and gender identification is a fluid, fragmented, dynamic hodgepodge of possibilities, and it may differ at different points in one's life. Queer theorists abhor binaries, especially the sex/gender binary. Probably the most famous American gender theorist, Judith Butler, who draws on the ideas of French philosopher Michel Foucault, argues that the body and sexuality are cultural constructs rather than natural phenomena. She claims that gender, far from being a biological fact, is a "performance."

Perform a behavior (femininity or masculinity) enough times and it begins to look like it is innate, but it is, in fact, an act.

But while psychoanalysis has not yet satisfactorily grappled with proliferating gender nonconformity either institutionally or theoretically, it has embraced the normalcy of diversity in sexual orientation. Yet this is only within the last thirty years. You merely have to glance at psychoanalytic journals of a few decades ago to find homosexuals described as overly narcissistic, perverted, arrested in their development, and/or incapable of mature love.

The trajectory of inclusion at psychoanalytic institutes is jagged. Let us use the Boston Psychoanalytic Society and Institute (BPSI) as an example. If we are to understand the integration of nonbinary persons into the BPSI fold, it is instructive to examine the integration of females and gays. To be sure, women were there at the beginning: Julia Deming, Lydia Dawes, Leolia Dalrymple, and later, Beata Rank, Helene Deutsch, Grete Bibring, Elizabeth Zetzel, and Eveoleen Rexford. But when I began my psychotherapy training in the Advanced Training Program in Psychoanalytic Psychotherapy (ATP) at BPSI in 1985, the ATP student body was almost entirely female, while our teachers, all psychoanalysts, were almost entirely male. Undoubtedly, this lopsided gender distribution reflected, in part, the nature of who went into which profession at that time: the ATP student group comprised mostly social workers and a few psychologists (then, often female), while the psychoanalyst candidate group was almost entirely made up of physicians (then, often male). Despite the fact that the feminist movement had started in the 1970s, internalized sexism remained strong in the 1980s, even among women, hampering them from pursuing professions dominated by men, or even contemplating such a move.

I clearly recall sitting in a program in the back of the auditorium at 15 Commonwealth Avenue (BPSI's home before Newton) and observing a sea of male balding heads. Psychoanalyst Anton Kris wrote in 2008 that BPSI in the 1980s had badly missed the boat:

It failed to note the changing circumstances of training, injured many colleagues, and deprived us of important fellow analysts until we were rescued by the great lawsuit that opened the doors of our Institute to psychologists and social workers and other clinicians with final degrees, under the Gaskill Amendment of the Bylaws of the American Psychoanalytic Association (APsaA) in 1986.

(Kris, 2008)

Regarding the presence of nonbinary persons as candidates or members of BPSI, there was no overt, written policy. My personal observation is that there were homosexual trainees in the ATP in the late 1980s, but they did not broadcast their sexual orientation. (The ATP, which began at BPSI in 1979, paved the way for more flexibility in training to meet personal and community needs.) Whether there were homosexual candidates for full psychoanalytic training then, I do not know. I am aware that a few openly gay candidates started in the 1990s. Paul Lynch, who in 1993 was one of two openly gay candidates (the other being Cary Friedman) to begin analytic training, said he thought that for most analysts, prejudice was born of life within a sheltered profession rather than active bigotry. "Many of these analysts didn't know a gay person as a friend or a social acquaintance, or somebody they were able to talk about it with outside of their offices," Lynch said to Erica Goode of the *The New York Times* (*The New York Times*, December 12, 1998).

Lynch's own experience when he entered the institute was positive. "I worried when I first joined that there were so few of us. But there really does seem to be a hunger for people to know more about this," he told the *Times*. In his second year of training, Lynch said, he realized negative attitudes toward gays laced much of the analytic literature he was reading for his analytical courses. When he raised the issue, the institute took steps to change the curriculum. "They really went to work and thanked me for exposing this," he added.

In 2003, Cary Friedman and Catherine Kimble led a seminar on gender and sexuality that I attended, along with joining the Ongoing Discussion Group on Sexual Orientation and Gender Identity, an offshoot of BPSI's Task Force on Gay and Lesbian Issues, co-sponsored by the Fenway Community Health Center and headed by analyst Gerry Adler. According to Lynch, the idea for the task force, which was joined by four or five faculty from BPSI, was to do "in-reach" as well as outreach to the gay community. Psychiatrist Larry Hartmann, who had been warned by his analyst of discrimination at BPSI, became a member of the discussion group. The sex/gender binary was starting to disintegrate. What was going on in Boston mirrored the earlier pioneering efforts of Ralph Roughton in the umbrella organization, APsaA. In 1991, it issued an antidiscrimination statement allowing training of gay psychoanalysts.

Let me put the Boston softening of a rigid sex binary into a broader perspective, for, as I noted in my book *The End of Gender: A Psychological Autopsy,* the binaries were disintegrating all over. By the 1960s, psychoanalytic theory, the theory that had taken sex out of the closet, became the one that had done much to keep it in—all but straight sex, that is. Originally revolutionary, the *agent provocateur* of the avant-garde (who then took dream life very seriously), psychoanalysis was literally mind-altering and antibourgeois. Psychoanalysts and creative types used to have an affinity for each other. Art and therapy circles seriously overlapped. The Hogarth Press, for example, was the first publisher of Freud in English. Hogarth was founded by Virginia and Leonard Woolf, who were part of a group of bohemian writers and thinkers known as the Bloomsbury Set.

Anaïs Nin, famous for her scandalous diaries, had been analyzed by Otto Rank. Salvador Dalí, for whom eccentricity was a stock-in-trade, painted the dream sequences reported by the psychiatric patient in Hitchcock's *Spellbound.* And lay analyst Lou Andreas-Salomé was the intimate of both philosopher Friedrich

Nietzsche and poet Rainer Maria Rilke. The list goes on. Visual artists like René Magritte and Man Ray, and modernist authors like James Joyce and William Faulkner, purposely tapped into the whirling thoughts and impulses of the unconscious, and architect Richard Neutra, like Freud, blurred the boundary between exterior and interior. Intellectual incest reigned. Artists and psychoanalytic therapists were mutually attracted allies in the cultural revolution.

But that was the art/psychoanalytic scene for the first half of the twentieth century. Psychoanalysis then calcified into a theory that, until thirty-five years ago, had been interpreted as sanctioning one, and only one, line of human development—that which leads to the heterosexual marital bed. It no longer smashed the status quo, but instead affirmed the conservative mindset of the "I Like Ike" era. It presupposed two complementary genders, each of which had an appropriate role and distinctive proclivities—in poet Adrienne Rich's words, "compulsory heterosexuality." The myopia of this view might not have been so damaging had parochial mid-century psychoanalytic thinking held less sway over the collective imagination. At the time, it powerfully influenced social science, education, child-rearing practices, and the law, as well as the psychotherapy business itself, and the very formation of psychiatric diagnostic categories. With its enormous prestige, it served to define what was healthy, good, and right; and "deviant" sexuality, and certainly "deviant" gender identity, did not qualify. What was once a liberating paradigm shift had itself become a repressive one.

By the 1990s, the scent of change (French perfume?) was in the air at the American Psychoanalytic Society (of which BPSI is a division). Importantly, its Executive Committee took a stand favoring the nondiscrimination of gays: it established workshops and discussion groups. This trickled down to Boston and other cities' institutes. But nonbinary gender was not on the radar screen.

Meanwhile, the Advanced Training Program at BPSI had been admitting gays all along, or, at least, in 1985, when I was a student. It is interesting to ponder why gay clinicians were deemed appropriate for psychotherapy training, but not for full-fledged psychoanalytic training. Perhaps it had to do with the juxtaposition of two lower-status groups: gays and folks who do psychotherapy (vs psychoanalysis). Perhaps, because the ATP was newer, it was not stuck in its ways. Or, perhaps it was freer to invent itself because there was no central or national organization.

As I wrote in the BPSI *Bulletin* in 2013, the BPSI members who founded the ATP in 1979—Judy Kantrowitz, Mort Newman, and Jim Dalsimer—did not anticipate that BPSI would change at its core by adding a psychotherapy training program (Thurer, 2013). The ATP had a modest beginning, housed in the former Extension Division, rather than emanating from the more prestigious Education Committee. Yet, even at that address, it had twice as many suitable applicants for the first class as spaces available. In those years, seasoned psychologists and social workers had no access, to my knowledge, to systematic psychoanalytic training of any kind in Boston, so the ATP tapped into a ready market.

But while the ATP attracted many applicants, it also stirred the pot—and provoked in-house ambivalence. Newman hinted at turf wars and status-mongering when he wrote in 2002 that some members of BPSI feared that graduates of the ATP would portray themselves as psychoanalysts. The history of the ATP at BPSI must be viewed in the context of the larger story of the complicated relationship between psychoanalysis and psychoanalytic psychotherapy. Most often, the relationship was euphemistically framed in intellectual or clinical terms, but those explanations mask some underlying tensions. (Alan Pollack has written thoughtfully about this subject.) Early on, many psychoanalysts considered psychoanalytic psychotherapy to be a knockoff. It was a treatment for those who could not tolerate psychoanalysis, or who could not afford the time or money. These hierarchical dynamics were mirrored by the organizational structures of the institutes, wherein psychotherapy programs were embedded as second-class citizens. Morton Newman oversaw the ATP in its early incarnation, joined later by Alan Pollack, who took the reins in 1988, functioning as director *avant la lettre* for twenty-four years. Pollack, a psychotherapy enthusiast, sought to upgrade its ranking on the BPSI organizational chart. Along with him, psychoanalysts Janet Noonan and José Saporta have worked to ensure that the stature of the ATP was equal to that of other BPSI programs. The pioneering ATP, with its open attitude towards homosexuality, paved the way, or at least functioned in a parallel manner, to the development of other programs at BPSI, thereby promoting intellectual cross-pollination, diversity, inclusion, and flexibility in training to meet personal and community needs.

Today, the atmosphere at BPSI is altogether more democratic, welcoming, and self-critical. All the BPSI programs now have trainees from all the sexual orientations. Binaries and status hierarchies have lost their importance. BPSI has recently joined APsaA in its apology to the LGBTQ+ community and pledged to eradicate racism and to foster diversity. The spring/summer 2018 issue of the BPSI *Bulletin* was "woke" to concerns of sexism and #MeToo, with various analysts conveying personal stories. Neither homosexuality nor nonbinary gender *per se* was addressed, but a liberalizing trajectory is clearly discernible. Heterosexuality is no longer a requirement for admission into the BPSI training program for becoming a full-fledged psychoanalyst. I suspect that BPSI will catch up with popular culture, and that folks like Caitlin Jenner, the character of ambiguous gender on *Billions*, or even the Teletubbies, may be considered for admission to training based on their qualifications, not their gender identification. *Salve* BPSI!

## Note

This essay deals primarily with attitudes toward gay males at BPSI. For thoughts on lesbian practitioners, see Chapter Nine, Gay women and the BPSI, p. 101.

## References

Beemyn, G., & Eliason, M. (forthcoming). *Campus Queer: Addressing the Needs of LGBTQ+ College Students* (Johns Hopkins University Press).

Centers for Disease Control and Prevention. (2019, January 24). *MMWR. Morbidity and Mortality Weekly Report.* https://www.cdc.gov/mmwr/index.html

Goode, E. (1998, December 12). On gay issue, psychoanalysis treats itself. *The New York Times.* https://www.nytimes.com/1998/12/12/arts/on-gay-issue-psychoanalysis-treats-itself.html

Hartocollis, A. (2020, February 19). Gender pronouns can be tricky on campus. *The New York Times.* https://www.nytimes.com/2020/02/19/us/gender-pronouns-college.html

Johns, M. M., Lowry, R., Andrzejewski, J., Barrios, L. C., Demissie, Z., McManus, T., Rasberry, C. N., Robin, L., & Underwood, J. M. (2019). Transgender identity and experiences of violence victimization, substance use, suicide risk, and sexual risk behaviors among high school students—19 states and large urban school districts, 2017. *MMWR. Morbidity and Mortality Weekly Report, 68*(3), 67–71. https://doi.org/10.15585/mmwr.mm6803a3

Kris, A. (2008, May 28). Remarks on the history of BPSI. *The BPSI Bulletin.*

Thurer, S. (2005). *The End of Gender: A Psychological Autopsy.* London: Routledge.

Thurer, S. (2013, Spring/Summer). The ATP story: A personal take. *The BPSI Bulletin.* https://bpsi.org/wp-content/uploads/2012/10/BPSIbulletinspring2013final.pdf

Vaughan, S. C. (2007). Scrambled eggs: Psychological meanings of new reproductive choices for lesbians. *Journal of Infant, Child, and Adolescent Psychotherapy, 6*(2), 141–155. https://doi.org/10.1080/15289160701624449

Vaughan, S. C. (2020, February). APsaA National Meeting.

Wolfe, E., & Ries, B. (2019, November 16). There are more LGBT characters on television than ever before. *CNN.* https://www.cnn.com/2019/11/16/entertainment/lgbtq-tv-representation-numbers-trnd/index.htmlcl

# CHAPTER TWO

# Being nonbinary

*Robin Haas*

*Without opposition there is no growth.*

—Daisaku Ikeda

I am Robin Haas. I am fifty-five years old, and an avid swimmer who, if given the chance, would gladly grow gills. In all serious-ness, I looked back and calculated that, before the pandemic, I had swum two and a quarter miles, 360 days each year, for over twenty years. My scent of choice is chlorine.

Since 2001, I have had a thriving private therapy practice, working with children, families, and adults. I supervise and train clinicians, have been on the Harvard teaching faculty, and am a life coach and a trainer and mentor for the Rhema group of coach-training schools. I am a member of NASW (National Asso-ciation of Social Workers), ACC (Associate Certified Coach), and the International Coach Federation (certified). Since 2008, I have been a Buddhist practitioner and a member of the Soka Gakki International.

I am also nonbinary.

My professional life fills me with joy. It always has. I started out studying at Boston University and graduated with a degree in elementary education. Studying child development and how people learn felt like a cakewalk to me. I am told that I was always studying people and was curious about what made them tick. What I did not like was being in a classroom. I thought I was just one of those people who fought the structure of the education system. However, I realize in retrospect that I like structure and discipline. After graduation I worked as a resident director at a small Catholic college near Boston, and then for the Massachusetts Department of Employment and Training. It was there that I got in touch with my clinical self and was encouraged by my mentor to study social work and become a clinician.

Interestingly enough, I had been considering law school or nursing school, but my mentor, who knew me better than I did myself, convinced me that social work was between nursing and law, so I applied to the Simmons School of Social Work, got in, and attended full time.

Simmons was a perfect fit for me. The curriculum provided an ideal balance between psychodynamic theory, narrative approaches, and practice. I felt I was finally part of something big, a legacy of the great minds of clinical work.

Despite this, I was not happy at that time. I hear this a lot: "I didn't think you ever had any problems, Robin. You seem so on top of things," or "You are one of the happiest people I know and so calm." Both are true, now, but that was not always the case. The truth is that I spent much of my life feeling isolated, alone, frightened, unsure, and uncertain.

Until a few years ago, I would have described myself as one of the shyest people you'd ever meet. This fact comes as a shock to many since I am a member of and trainer for the oldest LGBTQIA speakers' bureau in the United States.

Looking back on my life, there are a few things I have always known about myself. I love children. How and why things work (or do not work) fascinates me. Being an intuitive extrovert makes me well suited to work with others, and I am also comfortable working on my own. I am extremely curious and have always been creative, and thus prefer to figure it out than to be told how to do something. I have a passion for art, the arts, and the theater, and if I could sing, I would have wished to be on Broadway, or at least Off-Broadway.

I have always been a hard worker and have a propensity to want to do the right thing, get things correct, and I worry about ever making a mistake. I have at times been described as a perfectionist.

I was born in New York City, grew up in Connecticut, but from the very first time I set foot in Boston, I fell in love with the city that would someday become my home. I like the color blue, owls, the feel of wool, water, and I am a genuinely happy person. This last tidbit might surprise some when you learn that for much of my life I struggled with depression, suicidality, and my identity.

I was assigned female at birth. But I have known for as long as I can remember that I am not a girl. I have known that "girl" did not fit me.

Yet, it was not until about seven years ago that I came out to myself, when I realized I am nonbinary, that I no longer had to question who or what I was. Prior to that moment, every day felt like torture. I felt as if the rest of the world moved in sync and I was out of sync with it all.

So, how did it all begin, and how did I get here? Where is here, anyway?

As I mentioned, I started life as what people thought I was, a girl, and was given the name Robin Addison Haas, which is still the name I use. I do not remember consciously thinking that the gender I was assigned at birth was not my gender. Instead, I remember experiencing a constant, overriding sense that I did not fit in, anywhere.

My parents were high school graduates; my father was twenty years my mother's senior and had fought in World War II. He was a kind and gentle soul who had wanted more than anything to be a father, but he was told he could never biologically have a child. In the story of my life, that was not the first time medical science was wrong. My parents went on to have two more pregnancies; the first after me resulted in a stillbirth, and the next produced my brother, who is five years younger than I am.

I am told that from the moment my father learned of my mother's pregnancy with me, he became the happiest person on earth, and from the moment I was born, I was the apple of his eye. With him, I felt whole, loved, accepted, seen, and known.

We were a lot alike, and I wanted nothing more than to be just like my father. After the initial shock of his death when I was ten years old, my first thought was: "I now need to spend the rest of my life with a woman who does not know me and whom I do not know."

My mother is gifted, talented, creative, accepting, open, and brilliant. I just did not feel a sense of connection with her.

Being with my father was like being home! My family did not have rigid standards of modesty, and we lived in a "clothing optional" space if no one else was around. Before my brother was born, I looked at my body and envisioned it developing into one like my father's. My father and I enjoyed summer weekends fixing our boat, which was dry-docked for most of the summers. An old wooden fishing vessel that was more barnacle than boat, it required a lot of TLC, and it would be a long time before she would ever see water. My father and I spent hours and hours sweating in the hot sun getting "our" boat ready. When I got hot, my father took off my shirt, and I would go jump in Long Island Sound with all the other kids, mostly boys, at the boatyard. It was the early 1970s and most kids had long hair, as did I, and with shorts on, I looked like one of the boys.

I did not feel particularly different from the boys, but then again, I was four or five years old, and not many children think much about gender at that age.

Then, when I started kindergarten, my brother was born. I felt like my entire world fell apart. I felt as if I was tossed into a windstorm and got lost forever.

By the time my brother arrived, I was considered mature enough to help out with the new baby, and seeing his penis confused and frightened me. It was not that I had never seen a penis before, but rather that I had not seen one on me. I was born with what I imagined to be a tiny version of what would someday look like what my father had. I thought all I had to do was wait for it to grow. It never occurred to me that my body was destined to resemble my mother's. My chest was flat, it felt right and natural, and I felt a part of my father's club—the male club.

We talked openly, my father and I, and one day I asked him, "When will I grow one, a penis?" He smiled, hugged me, and explained a few facts about human anatomy and gender. His explanation satisfied me intellectually, but internally I was crushed.

To a five-year-old, everything you imagine yourself to be in your mind manifests as a physical picture. I had envisioned myself growing up looking much like I did at five, only a bit taller and with a penis. It made complete sense to me. When I was told that "my penis" would not grow, I was confused. I thought that there must be something wrong with "mine."

You might remember the Christmas special, *Rudolph the Red-Nosed Reindeer*? Rudolph is born to one of Santa's most famous reindeer, and it was believed he too would grow up to be strong and competent. Rudolph's parents, however, are shocked and embarrassed about their young child's oddity—a nose that glows.

Even the compassionate Santa suggests they cover it up, to avoid the horror of others seeing his truth. Rudolph soon shows how gifted he is, when he flies much earlier than his peers, but despite his precociousness, he is ostracized when he accidently reveals his bright red nose.

Eventually, Rudolph saves Christmas, leading Santa's sleigh through a big snowstorm. During the flight, they stop at the Island of Misfit Toys. There, he meets a Charlie-in-the-Box, a water pistol that squirts grape jelly, a cowboy that rides an ostrich, and a train with square wheels. I remember that something clicked all of a sudden while I was watching this movie. I liked that place. Everyone on that island had things that didn't fit. They all lived together while they waited to be seen and found. They waited for the day when they would be wanted by someone and freed from their island.

It was when I started kindergarten that I began to feel that I was destined to live a life on that kind of island, not worthy to be with others, not fitting in. This is what I remember about those first few days: I was forced to take naps when I wasn't tired. Having to lie down on a mat and rest was something I never did at home. I was active, always moving, and I still am. I go until I stop for the day. My energy does not slow simply because of a rule such as "it is nap time."

I soon figured out I could avoid nap time by requesting permission to use the lavatory.

This was a large single-occupancy room inside my kindergarten class. It was soundproof, with a heavy solid-core door, and large enough to provide a perfect amount of play space. While my classmates napped, I would escape to my own private playroom. I would craft stories and act them out with imaginary friends or play with small toys I would bring from home. That was all I needed to entertain myself for the entire nap period.

The other thing I remember happening at the start of kindergarten was being introduced to the concept that there were two groups of people—boys and girls.

At the very beginning of the first day of school, the teacher showed the class where the girls' coats were to be hung and where the boys' coats were to be hung. It was still warm in New England, and I wasn't wearing a coat, so I did not give this practice much thought.

Then the teacher told us to line up, girls in one line, boys in the other. In that one moment, my world started to become very small. The other students immediately moved into whichever line they belonged, and I stood in what felt like the outskirts of my world. I had no idea where to go, and they did. In my way of thinking, all the other students must have been told by their parents where to go when instructed like this, but no one had told me.

When you are five and other people know something and you don't, they belong and you don't.

I asked the teacher, "Where do I go?" The expression on her face frightened me. She looked at me in a way that told me to never, ever question something like this again. My five-year-old mind told me that I had done something very wrong. But I couldn't figure out what. I had followed the rules, hadn't I? And still, I caused trouble.

Then the teacher pointed me toward the line of other students dressed like me.

At that time, little girls wore dresses and little boys wore pants, and the implication was that I was a little girl. So, I lined up with the kids who wore dresses, and in that line I stayed, not because I knew I was a girl, but because I was told that was how others perceived me.

We come to know and understand who we are in relation to others. Sometimes the messages we receive are direct, such as: *You are smart,* or *You are lazy.* At other times, those messages are delivered indirectly. Always being chosen last for the kickball team might come to mean you are not a good player or you are not wanted. We grow up interpreting these messages and creating stories in our minds about who and what we are, and those stories become ingrained. If the story is affirming and positive, and aligns with how we feel, life can seem pretty good. However, when stories are limiting and negative, or are in contrast with how we feel, life can become uncertain and confusing.

Until kindergarten, I did not have to think of myself as belonging in a girls' line, or a boys' line. I did not have to think about belonging to any group. I had felt part of my family, I was part of a neighborhood. I was a person who could help repair a boat. I played with those who felt themselves to be boys and those who felt themselves to be girls. I enjoyed the freedom of moving from one group to the other. I had not felt a need to be one or the other, and no one else classified me as either. Being forced to stay with one gender immediately felt wrong to me.

In that one moment in kindergarten, I went from being me to being a person that was *not, neither*, and somehow wrong. I could tell by the look on my teacher's face that I was very, very wrong. My feelings of fear and confusion became almost intolerable, but it was the shame that rendered me powerless and stuck. From that time on, I hated going to school. I had no one to play with. I had no allies. I felt I didn't belong and would never belong. Very quickly, a deep sense of hopelessness set in.

Over the next few years, I tried to fit myself into groups of my peers. I watched as others seemed to find their places among those who looked or dressed like they did. There was no place that felt like the warm hug of my father or the safety of my bedroom, where I could just be me.

I tried to figure myself out, but everywhere I turned did not fit me and I did not fit it. I started to fear going to sleep because in the morning things probably would be the same and I would still feel lost. I worried about with whom I could play and how I was supposed to act. My family would tease me about being a worrywart. I even had a character doll that looked half monster, half Muppet. It wore a sign that read: I AM A WORRYWART, DON'T WORRY ME.

But I did worry, all the time. And the more I tried to blend in, the more confused I felt about what I was. I felt I was destined to be alone, never fitting in.

It got even worse after a terrifying incident at a museum in New York City.

My mother, father, and I were all born in the city, and my maternal grandparents lived there until their deaths. Our family moved to the suburbs when I was an infant. The problem was, my mother felt most at home in New York City, and unlike other children, we spent many of our summers there. Despite loving nature, trees, and the safety and seclusion of my own bedroom, I actually did not mind our time in New York all that much because my mother seemed happier and more at ease being in what she must have considered home.

Another reason was that my grandmother and I had a special routine that helped me, in a way, feel more normal. My mother usually spent her days shopping and my grandmother would take us to the park, after which we'd have a snack. We'd get to pick a treat from the corner store or the bakery where we stopped for bread. This was special because at home we were not permitted to have sweets. My mother was terrified that her daughter would get fat. The other kids got to bring cream-filled cupcakes wrapped in cellophane in their school lunches, but I was not allowed to have these treats. However, on these outings I could eat what the other kids had, and then I could share in the chatter on the playground, noting that my favorites were Yodels. We had something in common.

In the city, there was also the pleasure of watching my grandfather get ready for work. He worked for the United States Postal Service and took his presentation very seriously. I saw him iron his work shirts, putting them on, carefully buttoning them up and folding down the collar. I admired his pressed slacks and freshly starched shirts. I always thought that he was doing something very important to have to wear such a carefully prepared wardrobe. I could not wait to grow up and do something that required me to wear a shirt like his, and if it required a tie like my father's work did, even better!

Then one day I actually got to dress like a boy! I was about eight or nine, and we were going to a museum. Usually on such an outing we had to dress up, but this time was different. My mother put my brother and me in tracksuits, the kind with the matching pants and jacket with wide white stripes down the pant legs and sleeves. My suit was blue and my brother's was red. I was thrilled to be wearing what he wore. I think my mother's affinity for these tracksuits outweighed any rules she may have had about the correct attire to visit a museum. Since these were tracksuits, I got to wear my sneakers too!

There is no way for me to convey the significance of what I wore that day other than to suggest that you consider the significance a royal family might place on the proper attire for, let's say, a wedding. It meant so much to me that I was wearing honest-to-goodness boys' clothing, and everything felt just right. In my mind, I was the big brother that day, and moving through the world felt effortless, until …

… I had to use the bathroom.

By that time, I had proven myself capable of going to the restroom on my own, so my mother pointed me in the direction of the ladies' room. She said she would stay with my brother at the exhibit so I'd not worry or get lost when I came out.

Off I headed, and within a few moments I heard: "Little boys don't belong in the little girls' room." At first, it sounded like a whisper, but then it got louder and louder. I was not sure if I was saying it to myself or if someone else was saying it to me. I turned around and there, now in front of me, was an elderly woman pointing her finger in my face and yelling repeatedly, *Little boys don't belong in the little girls' room!*

I was terrified and ran into an empty stall. Afterward, washing my hands, who should be standing next to me but that very same woman. Her words were quieter now, but I could certainly make them out: "Little boys don't belong in the little girls' room."

By the time I got back to my mother, I was in tears. I was terrified. I shared the experience; my mother hugged me and told me to ignore the woman. This I remember distinctly, my mother said that *the woman did not know what she was talking about.*

For any other youngster, I suspect, the words of a mother trying to comfort her traumatized child would have been helpful. But there was something much deeper going on for me.

Here I was, a kid, not sure what gender I was. The fact I was directed to the ladies' room did not seem strange. That is where my mother always took both my brother and me while we were out of the house. In those days, major department stores had a "ladies' lounge"—code for *bathroom*. In fact, there were toilet stalls, but before you got to them you walked through what felt like a long corridor. The corridor opened up to large room with comfy sofas and chairs and huge mirrors, and they always smelled like perfume and powder. I loved that room; I could climb on the sofas, and sit and read and take a break from the dreaded activity of the day—shopping.

I hated shopping; I still do.

But my visit that day was not fun. On that day I heard the words I feared most—*You don't belong.*

It was one thing for me to *think* I did not belong, but for another person to point to me and tell me directly that I did not belong felt like a confirmation of my worst fears. By the time I got back to my mother, my balloon had popped. Though I was not sure where I belonged, I had in many ways felt myself to be a boy. According to this woman, I was a boy. And, I felt sure I was not a girl.

The fact is, I now sensed I was neither a girl nor a boy. So I must be nothing, and I knew there was no space and no place for a person like me. This became my secret, my hidden identity, and until I could figure out what I was, there would be no place for me.

On the Island of Misfit Toys, all the toys had a part that didn't fit. The difference for me was that it wasn't just one part, it was all of me that didn't fit. I wasn't even "misfit" enough to live on their island.

And so, there I was, on my island all by myself. I started to create an entire world based on what I thought was true for me, that there was no place for me. That was the story I kept telling myself. Every experience had to fit that narrative. Otherwise, I felt more and more lost.

Because I did not have a lot of friends, I could spend a lot of time focusing on schoolwork, and I did well academically. No one really knew I didn't have many friends. My parents thought I did because I could talk about what this person did in school that day, or what that person brought for lunch, but in reality, I did not spend much time with others on the playground or in the lunchroom. Those spaces were for girls or boys.

On the playground boys gathered to play kickball. They told me the game was for boys and asked me to leave. The girls played four square or played house. I always wanted to be the father, and they were playing only mothers, so I left the group and sat by myself.

No teacher seemed to pay attention to how sad I was, but truth be told, I never said anything about it. I did not know what to say. There were no words to express the feeling of being neither a girl nor a boy, the feeling of not fitting in.

Since I was praised for my schoolwork, I thought I must be a "good student" and defined myself that way. There wasn't anything bad about doing well in school. The trouble started when being a good student became the only way I defined myself. Getting perfect scores became the measure of my self-worth. Teachers commented with pride when I got things right. When I got something wrong, they would say how surprised they were. I took that to mean I had let them down.

Here is how my narrative went: If I got good grades, that meant I was a good person. It meant people liked me, it meant things were going to be all right. If I got a bad grade, I would fall into a state of deep despair. It meant I was bad, wrong, a failure, that I was a source of disappointment. I could know, just by looking at my work for the day, how good I was. I needed to do well or else my world would crumble. If I made a mistake on a test, I would plead with teachers to let me do make-up work to bring up my grade to that same perfect place. They would usually let me. I learned I could control my grades and therefore my sense of self.

After a while, teachers and my mother would tell me to stop worrying so much about my grades, that no one expected me to get perfect scores all the time. But that was not true—I did. I needed to do well in school because that was the only way I could know who I was. I no longer needed to know if I was a boy or a girl. I had a new identity: the skinny kid who got good grades.

It felt comforting to know I had some control over who I was or, rather, who I told myself I was. Then I felt I had control over how others perceived me.

But eventually I became obsessed with my inner world and what exactly I could control. If things stayed the same, if I got the same grades, things made sense. If not, my world would fall apart.

Still, even when I did well academically, nothing felt natural or easy. People would comment on things I did, saying they were odd. I liked art, my peers liked clothes and the latest fashion trends. My peers liked male teen pop stars and I didn't. I remember when one of the neighborhood kids my age told me I was dumb for not liking Erik Estrada (the teen heartthrob at the time). She told me there was something wrong with me if I didn't want to kiss him and said she was asking for an Erik Estrada poster for Christmas and that I should do the same if I wanted to be in their club.

I went home and asked for the poster, hoping this would bring me closer to being part of my peer group. I thought that somehow when I got my poster, something inside of me would click and I'd figure out how to be, how to act in the world. On some level, I knew my thinking was erroneous, but it didn't matter because at that time, it was all I had to guide me.

Christmas came, I got the poster, hung it in my room, and still no one liked me. Clearly, they had forgotten about the test they'd given me, and when I rose to the challenge, they all left me, alone. Having that poster made me no more than what I felt I was—nothing.

Through all this time, it was not as if no one had noticed I was troubled. I had seen a therapist—but it was not about trying to decide who I was. It was about losing my father.

I was devastated when my father died. He had been the only person who I felt understood me. I considered us to be kindred spirits. Without him, I believed there was not a single person on the planet who would ever understand me. His death marked a death, at that time, for me.

When my grief lasted longer than I suppose my mother thought it should have, I was sent to therapy. I cannot say that therapy was not helpful. I went for years. My therapist helped me deal with losing my father, and when they suggested we stop, I figured I was healed—or that I should act like it.

One way therapy did help was that it gave me the words I needed to describe my internal experiences. Words like "depressed" and "despondent" resonated with me. When I used them in therapy, my therapist seemed to know how to direct our conversation. My takeaway from therapy was that I was depressed, but it still left me feeling no more certain of who I was. Until about eight years ago, I would wake up every morning wondering if I was male or female.

The next time I was sent to therapy it was for an eating disorder, which started after I got my period. Whenever I talk with people about growing up nonbinary, they always ask about puberty, assuming it must be torture for any trans person. Well, I cannot speak for anyone but me, but quite honestly for me, being assigned female but actually being nonbinary, I just felt female puberty had no place in my life.

When I was about thirteen years old, my body started changing, or "developing" as my mother would say. I noticed hair growing under my arms, and that did not bother me at all. My chest started to grow, as did my hips and thighs, and I needed to shop in the girls' department for pants and shirts. I was a small person, I still am, so I never really made it to the women's department—that is, not until I started gaining weight.

I remember that I was mortified when I got my period. It was just wrong, so very wrong. How could this happen to someone who was not a girl? I felt doomed, I felt as if my life was over, I felt as if I had somehow caused this event to occur, and that if I was truly not a girl, then somehow, I would have been able to avoid it.

Whether or not I got my period also became the obsession of others. I only got it once or twice and then it stopped. I was taken to the doctor. Medical professionals became worried, and I was put on birth control to force my body into full-fledged female puberty. Then I felt totally out of sync with my body. All I wanted to do was crawl out of my skin. Everything felt wrong internally, physiologically. Externally, everything was wrong because my body responded to the surge of female hormones. My body grew curves. I gained weight. I blamed myself for growing breasts and hips and thighs, and was ashamed of my own inability to maintain the body I was *supposed* to have.

I had heard that people who had grown too large could go on a diet of their own volition and lose weight. I figured that if it was my fault for growing, it was up to me to control my shape. I tried to stop taking the pill but the doctors ordered me to continue. Because I was a compliant people pleaser, I did as I was told. But since no one said I could not go on a diet, I did. My weight and size became my new obsession.

Being the determined perfectionist that I was, I learned that in addition to academics, dieting was something else I was good at. I would starve myself to the point that I had no chest and hips, thinking my body's shape would lead me to the answer. When that didn't work, I'd eat and eat, and double my size so that I'd get hips and breasts, thinking that would tell me what I was. Being with others felt like pressure to pick "boy" or "girl," and that was all I could focus on.

So I went to therapy again. The focus of that treatment was on my eating, or lack thereof. My mother would tell me that most kids my age got involved with drugs, and why couldn't I just do that, because *that* she could understand. As much as I hated to admit it, I wished the same thing. If I was "only" addicted to drugs, my turmoil would cease once I received the prescribed treatment, and my torture would end. Now I know that is not true. The path to any kind of recovery is long, steep, and not easy for anyone, but at least substance abuse had a name. It had a group of people afflicted with it, and there was a way out. I saw no way off my lonely island.

I finally gave up trying to figure it out—or tried to give up. I was told I was a girl, so that is what I would resign myself to being. Acting was something at which I was skilled, so I practiced being a girl.

That continued when I went away to college. But trying to live as a girl, trying to fit in but feeling lost, I was so isolated and depressed that I couldn't focus on school. So I dropped out after my first year. Eventually I became suicidal, and my mother made me go to therapy as a condition for staying out of school.

I knew I was attracted to girls, so I told the therapist that I was gay. To me, it was easier to talk about sexuality than gender, and

doing so, I could feel somewhat normal. Didn't other people struggle with coming out as gay? Unfortunately, my therapist's response
was: "Well, since you haven't had sex with anyone, there is no way
for you to know for sure, so I think maybe you are not gay." The
interesting thing was that I hadn't asked her if I was gay or not,
I just said I was. I was not upset about it. Her reaction, however,
confirmed for me that I could not raise the issue of gender. If being
gay was off the table, then having been assigned the wrong gender
at birth was not a topic I could bring up.

I terminated therapy as soon as I could.

I spent a year working a number of jobs and made friends with
some of the people I met at a summer camp. I loved kids and took
a job at the Jewish Community Center in their nursery school and
day care center. I also ran some of the children's programs and
helped out with the set design and production of the children's
play. The director of the play and I became friends. He was gay,
and about ten or fifteen years older than I was, but I felt connected
to and accepted by him, and in a lot of ways, I identified with him.
Our connection never felt in any way sexual. To me, it just felt like
two dudes hanging out. After the children's play, he asked me to
join him in his work directing a community theater production
for the town where I lived. I think my mother thought I had a
crush on him and told me he was gay and that I should not get my
hopes up. When I told her it never occurred to me to want to date
him and that he was one of the first people I ever felt understood
me and liked me, she seemed glad that I finally had a friend.

I know that it was not his gayness that comforted me, it was
his "maleness" that did, but still, I had no words for what I felt.
I remember thinking maybe my mother was right, maybe what
I felt toward men was an attraction to them, and not an attraction to be like them. At any rate, meeting someone with whom I
could connect must have helped me feel less uncomfortable about
being me.

I decided to go back to school, and I was able to make it through the next two and a half decades or so of my life. I managed to graduate from Boston University with a bachelor of science degree in elementary education and a minor in sociology. By the time I graduated, I realized I wanted to know and study how people learned, worked, made decisions, and came to feel whole.

While at school I met the person who was to become my best friend and soul mate for life. Steve and I met through a mutual friend with whom I worked a few campus catering jobs the summer between my junior and senior years. When we met, things just clicked for us. Steve and I were finishing each other's sentences within a week of meeting. We ended up dating, fell in love, and broke up when he came out as gay. His coming out did not change our friendship at all. For a long time, there was no Steve without Robin, no Robin without Steve.

Although we met in 1988, it feels as if there has never been a time when we have not known each other, nor been in each other's lives. We have lived on opposite sides of the country for many years now, and still people think of us as one. I can remember going to one of our favorite vacation spots by myself. While having a drink at a bar, I struck up a conversation with someone who commented that while I obviously was not a gay man, I reminded him so much of someone he'd met there earlier that summer. Without missing a beat, I said, "Oh yes, that was Steve. He's my brother." I honestly did not know Steve had been there, but there is no one else in this world who is more like me.

Steve taught me how to laugh. The first time I laughed, really laughed, was when I was about twenty. I'd tried, and I learned how to fake it and make a good show for others, but it was never deep or real. I could stop faking with Steve. He has always accepted me, and in his eyes, I am whole. Steve taught me to embrace life fully, and he showed me what unconditional love is all about. I learned that being as honest with oneself and with others, as honest as we can be in any given moment, creates the fertile ground necessary for love and intimacy.

When Steve came out to me as gay, I never had to worry about our friendship. We separated as romantic partners, but never as best friends. I learned that nothing could separate friends, and Steve worked very hard to prove to me how much he loved the person I was and am. After about a year, I found myself more and more attracted to women, and came out as gay.

Steve's reaction was unexpected for sure. Steve was surprised. It shocked me that he did not know. Until that point, I thought we could read each other's minds. His explanation makes perfect sense, however. I had no female friends. All of our friends were guys, and most or all of them were gay men. Many people made the assumption that I was attracted to gay men when, in actuality, I identified with them, that is, with being male. Around groups of women, I felt like an impostor because it was assumed I was one of them, when I wasn't. With men, although I did not feel fully male, I did not have to pretend I that was. There was no impostor feeling, and I felt part of the group.

At some point shortly after coming out, I reconciled my confusion about my own gender and came up with a theory. I figured that if I liked women, and people thought I was a female, it must follow that all who define themselves as gay women must also be confused about their gender. I thought it was a part of being gay.

Then one day about six or seven years ago, I was having dinner with a colleague and friend. Both of us are clinicians who work with transgender and gender nonconforming kids and adults. We got to talking about coming out, gender, and identity. Over the course of the evening, my friend commented about how good it felt to be with women; to hang out with, to stand up with women; to *be* a woman. She said that when she realized she was gay and called herself a lesbian, everything just felt right. My friend talked about this feeling of being with others who you just knew understood you, who were *like* you. She said that in female spaces she felt she was home. I think she even may have said she felt stronger as a person calling herself a lesbian.

It occurred to me at that moment that not all gay women woke up each day wondering if they were male or female. I had come to think that my gender and my sexuality were interrelated, that feeling "not a girl" was what it meant to be gay.

"You mean *you* don't wake up every morning wondering if you are a boy or a girl?" I asked her.

The question surprised me more than it did my friend. She looked at me with kindness and compassion and said, "No, sweetie, but my wife does."

I'd met her wife, a loving soul, shy, introverted, and someone, I'd been told, who does not open up to people easily, a fact I found strange because she and I hit it off well right from the start.

And in one very powerful transformative moment, I realized who I am, what is true for me. I realized I am not the only person who wakes up sometimes feeling like a girl, sometimes like a boy, and sometimes like neither. I am nonbinary. Now someone saw me on my island and invited me to the mainland, knowing who I was. She saw me and accepted me when I hadn't even given myself permission to do that.

When I first came out, a few people called me a lesbian. I corrected them and told them, "No, I am gay." Now I know why I strongly resisted that label. I am not female, and a lesbian is a woman, and I am not …

That experience was transformative, but it did not erase the pain and suffering I had endured. I had grown up feeling wrong in my own body, with a deep sense of shame. None of that was going away all at once.

When I was young, my father used to tell me that living a good life meant being able to wake up in the morning, look in the mirror, and say, "I like and respect that person," and be able to do the same going to bed at night. His words were embedded in my soul, and I wanted so badly to look in the mirror and say I liked and respected myself.

From the experience of being told to get in the girls' line, I believed I was flawed and wrong. The experience of being told that little boys don't belong in the little girls' room taught me that I didn't belong. If my whole life had been based on pretending to be something I am not, how could I like and respect myself as an adult?

I have learned to do that through my Buddhist practice. I learned about the true nature of our lives. Buddhism teaches that our lives are eternal and that inherent in each of us is the noble and enlightened state of Buddhahood. No matter our background, our gender, our history, physical makeup, or status in society, we are equally worthy of the utmost respect. Not only that, it teaches that in order to access this enlightened state, we have to challenge and overcome the negative tendencies that can rule us and plunge us into suffering.

I am a member of the Soka Gakkai International, the lay organization of Nichiren Daishonin Buddhist practitioners. A key concept in Nichiren Buddhism is "casting off the transient and revealing the true." We can transcend our provisional state of existence and courageously bring forth the true state of our lives. When I first started practicing, I studied and sought guidance and worked to infuse my life with this concept, casting off what was not true about myself in order to reveal my inner truth. I could not get to that truth until I identified what was not, and understood that trying to be something I was not is what led me to living in hell. Once I could see what was real about me, I could live my reality.

Also helpful has been *The Work* of Byron Katie, which begins with bringing awareness to your thoughts. Katie, as she is familiarly known, teaches that discomfort or stress comes from an attachment we hold to something that is not true. I have learned how to question the beliefs that kept me limited and painfully unhappy, and to turn them around to reveal what is truer about myself and my life.

One example is the shame I felt for gaining weight: gaining weight was what led to having breasts, and that was all my fault. Applying *The Work* to this belief, I could ask if that was a true statement. Exploring this further, I could see that it is not true, it is not my fault I have breasts. I could also see that it is my thinking that is telling me it is my fault. I can change my thinking and believe I am not at fault. Not only am I not at fault, having breasts does not mean I am a girl. Body shape and size are not indicators of my gender nor of anyone's gender.

Practicing identifying what is not true for me is a daily process that has led to freedom. I can wear what I want, and nothing that I wear dictates my gender. Sometimes I feel like wearing clothing that makes me look more traditionally boy, and sometimes I choose to wear clothing that makes me look more traditionally girl. To me, gender is not a thing, or a category, it is a feeling.

When I told my mother I was nonbinary, she responded by asking if she should call me her child instead of her daughter. I thought, "Yup," and that was it. That was all I needed, to be seen and heard, and not questioned. Her response was an indication of acknowledgment and acceptance. She and I can talk openly about gender because she is not trying to view my gender through her own cis gender lens.

I have an aunt with whom I am very close, and she struggles with my pronouns. She was a teacher for many years, and says that, to her, "they" is plural. She also struggles with what to call me when she introduces me to friends. "Niece does not work," she tells me. "Nephew" does not work for me. I wish we had nongendered titles for relatives, but we do not, so I suppose we will need to create them. As for a title for me, I have not identified one, so my aunt just calls me Robin, because that is my name, and it is what I ask to be called. Sometimes my mother will call me Rob, and I am just fine with that.

As for "they/them," well, perhaps these words have been used to refer to more than one of something, but words take on new meanings and spellings all the time. I could also add that people already use "they" in reference to an individual. When we are behind a slow driver, one who seems uncertain about which turn to make, we might say, "They don't know where they're going." We say that even if we can see that there are no others in the car. The driver is one person and we refer to them as "they."

To any person who tells me there is no way I will be able to convince them that "they" can be used as a singular pronoun, I tell them that is fine with me. I am in no way trying to convince anyone of anything. I just prefer that people use these pronouns for me. It is simply a respectful thing to do, to refer to a person by their name and their preferred pronouns. (*I encourage you to make note of the pronouns I used in this paragraph.*)

For those who struggle to remember to use my pronouns, I suggest practicing. Just do it, at home, while you are out, in the presence of others, just practice. Say: "There goes Robin, they're running at a good clip," or "Robin said they'd like to watch a movie tonight."

No one knows for sure what makes a person trans, or nonbinary, any more than what makes a person cis. If we rely on medical science and genetics, we know that hormones are the determining factors in the shape of our bodies and the functioning of our reproductive systems and organs. Do hormones make a person feel one gender or the other? I don't think we know, because we are thus far unable to construct a controlled study for psychosexual development. To do so would involve the impossible task of raising a child in an environment that is absent of all stereotypes, expectations, cultural contexts, and assumptions.

If we do not yet have scientific explanations, at least we have more openness and awareness, more visibility. More people are coming out as trans and nonbinary. Seeing others who are representative of who we are can help reduce feelings of being wrong or different. Now therapists are trained to ask, "Which pronouns do you use?" or "Have you ever thought the gender you were assigned at birth is not accurate?" or even, "When did you first realize gender existed?"

If I had been invited to consider gender in those many sessions with my therapists, I might have let myself wonder about it more openly. The message would have been: gender can be questioned, and there is nothing wrong with doing so.

It is important to ask clients who identify as nonbinary what that means to them. It may be different for others, but to me, I am not partly a boy and partly a girl. I am nonbinary. Nonbinary is a gender unto itself.

Knowing this now has brought me a sense of freedom and, finally, a sense of belonging in the world. I can live my life without limits and feel in alignment with who I really am.

# CHAPTER THREE

# A clinical reflection on "Being nonbinary" by Robin Haas

*Rita Teusch*

I am very grateful to Robin for sharing with us what it was like for them to grow up nonbinary.

I am a cisgender woman and a psychoanalyst who has treated several patients of different genders with psychoanalysis, including an individual who identifies as nonbinary and whose painful feelings and experiences growing up were similar to Robin's. I have also supervised psychoanalytic candidates who were treating nonbinary patients in analysis, and I am familiar with the complex ways in which painful childhood feelings and experiences infuse feelings and fantasies about the self, which are reinforced by messages, attitudes, and experiences prevalent in our society. Analysts have the privilege to learn from patients of different genders in the privacy and safety of the consulting room. However, honest and insightful first-person narratives such as

Robin's allow us all to become educated about and aware of the internal and external challenges that those who grow up feeling that they do not fit in with societal gender expectations are faced with every day.

Historically, individuals of different genders have often not been visible or have not felt empowered to share their painful experiences and feelings. Perhaps an increasing openness about gender variations and greater visibility have allowed more people of different genders to come forward with their stories. However, our society and our helping profession still have a long way to go in terms of educating ourselves about the negative emotional impact that can be the result of a highly gender-focused socialization, especially for children.

Robin Haas has worked on themself for many years to overcome their painful feelings associated with growing up nonbinary. They had some help from therapists, but mostly they were left on their own to figure out how to live and succeed in a society which was not open to different genders, especially when they were in their formative years. Robin was able to gain a perspective on their life-long suffering because of family support, intelligence, emotional strength, multiple talents, creativity, and ability to be psychologically minded and self-reflective. Reading their autobiographical account, I felt deep admiration for Robin's ability to persist, struggle, survive, reach out, thrive, and eventually also find peace and happiness after many years of suffering painful confusion, anxiety, guilt, and shame because they were nonbinary.

Robin's account is powerful and speaks for itself. I will highlight a few of their internal and external experiences that struck me as crucial, the pain of which might have been alleviated had they encountered a greater awareness of and sensitivity to gender diversity from the people and institutions they interacted with.

Robin's first conscious memory of "not fitting in" was the moment in kindergarten when they realized that they did not fit in with the girls' line nor were they allowed to stand in the boys' line. We can assume that this was a traumatic moment for Robin, because until then they had felt mostly comfortable playing with the boys, and their family had accepted them and allowed them to do and play in the way they felt comfortable, in other words, hang out with their father and the boys in the boatyard. The binary gender norms they encountered in kindergarten introduced Robin to formal gender-based rules, and they felt this was the official beginning of their feeling deeply confused and ashamed of themself, and needing to hide their true feelings about who they were, that they fit in better with the boys, and that they did not feel they were a girl. Robin's childhood mind interpreted this as being "wrong," flawed, and defective as a person. We may submit that Robin was also confused around this time when they saw the penis of their brother, who was born at that time. Like many children, they remembered thinking that their own "small penis" will eventually grow.

The next traumatic scene for Robin was the scene in the restroom at age eight or nine, when their mother had dressed them and their brother alike, in boys' clothing. Robin had felt on top of the world because they enjoyed being dressed like a boy because it felt right to them. When they were told by a woman that "little boys don't belong in the little girls' room," they felt further confusion and shame. Their mother tried to comfort them, but Robin felt devastated. Robin had found comfort by seeing themself as belonging to the Island of Misfit Toys, but after the restroom incident, they felt they no longer belonged among the misfit toys because they were missing not just one part that was a misfit, but their whole self was "wrong." I remember that my nonbinary patient was deeply convinced that they were a "mutant," not fully human, which expressed their profound shame, pain, and alienation.

At age ten, Robin lost their father, the person they had felt closest to, totally accepted by, and whole with, and this loss was devastating for them. As Robin later realized, they themself "died with him." Robin began to feel profoundly untethered, alone, lonely, and even more confused about how to act and who they really were. They knew they could not live out or even express their true feelings, and, subsequently, they developed a false self, "a pretend life," in other words, a self that was based on what they believed others wanted them to be. We know from other mental health conditions that a lack of positive affirmation of the true self, which is also associated with a harsh superego ("you did something wrong, you are bad"), forces the patient into a false-self adaptation with serious consequences for their further development. Luckily, Robin's mother sent them to therapy, and they received some help with developing a language to deal with their father's death and their anxiety and depression. Perhaps today, in a more open climate with regard to gender, the therapist might have noticed some of their confused or shameful feelings about gender and would have encouraged them to express and explore them.

Over time, Robin began to realize that they could excel and get approval by achieving excellent grades, and their good grades became an obsession and began to replace for a while their worry about gender. Robin continued to feel lonely, trying to fit in sometimes with others, but mainly giving up trying to fit in because it felt impossible. They entered puberty, and getting their period and feeling their body change was greatly anxiety-provoking, and they felt more and more out of control. Robin developed anorexia nervosa, an illness common in individuals who were psychologically forced to develop a false self. Restricting food initially increased their sense of control, also with regard to the shape of their body, especially since having breasts had increased their guilt and shame. Robin was put on birth control pills to regulate their cycle, but the side effects led to intense physical discomfort, further increasing their feelings of powerlessness, and leading to suicidal feelings. We know that the death rate of nonbinary and transgender individuals, either by suicide or murder, is steadily growing. At least twenty-eight transgender people were murdered, or their death was suspicious, in the first seven months of 2019, compared to twenty-six the whole year before. According to data collected by the National Center for Transgender Equality, twenty-three of the victims were transgender women, four were transgender men, and one was nonbinary. The epidemic of violence is particularly pronounced for Black and Latina trans women.

Robin dropped out of college after their first year because they felt unable to function, depressed, and painfully different from their peers. They sought therapy again, this time their eating disorder being the focus, and Robin was left with the impression that food and eating were acceptable topics for therapy, but their thoughts about gender were taboo.

Reading this gender autobiography, I felt sad. Having treated many patients with eating disorders in the 1980s and 1990s, I knew how often an eating disorder was missed by clinicians during that time, even anorexia, which is more noticeable than bulimia and compulsive overeating. Clearly, the topic of gender was another taboo and was not spoken about openly. Robin's therapist was able to help them with their eating disorder, but discouraged the exploration of their feelings about gender ("you have not had sex so you don't know if you are gay or not"). I hope this has changed in 2022, but unfortunately, patients may still today encounter attitudes from therapists and analysts that betray lack of knowledge about gender diversity.

We need education about gender diversity to feel comfortable reaching out and encouraging our patients to discuss their feelings about and experiences with their gender. Just as we have learned from patients with eating disorders: it is often not until the therapist actively brings up the issue that a patient will feel comfortable enough to begin to reveal their internal struggles. The same is true of gender issues because the shame and guilt that are generated by not fitting into societal norms have a paralyzing effect and often require the patient to dissociate from these feelings if they want to continue with their lives.

When Robin started, in their twenties, to get to know openly gay people, they began to feel less alone and more connected. They found a close gay friend with whom they fell in love and who became their soul mate. They felt well enough then to go back to finish undergraduate school and then attend graduate school. As Robin stated: It was not the sexual attraction that was most important, but rather this person's maleness, which, it seems, reawakened in Robin the deep comfort they had known when being with their father.

But Robin still had not yet fully understood that they were nonbinary. This only happened when they met the partner of a lesbian friend who felt like Robin; wondering every day whether they were a boy or a girl and wondering how to behave every day, like a boy or a girl, and trying to find ways to fit in with society and their peers. Robin had felt some affinity with gay people, but had also realized that their own emotional experience was different from that of most gay people. Robin did not feel that what they were concerned with was about sexual preference. The meeting with their lesbian friend's partner was transformative for Robin because they had finally found someone who had similar feelings to their own: They were both struggling with not feeling that the gender they were assigned at birth was the right one that fit their experience of themselves and that they identified with. Their gender identity was such that neither gender felt right; in other words, they did not belong to either the male or the female gender.

After coming out as nonbinary, Robin could begin to ask for the support they needed, asking people close to them for their respect, including using the pronouns that they felt most accurately described their self-experience. Feeling finally that they did not have to pretend any longer to be either a girl or a boy felt like a huge relief. They could now let their feelings about themselves guide their life, including their gender presentation; in other words, sometimes they felt and dressed more like a male and sometimes like a female. With the help of Buddhist practice, Robin further recovered and found a sense of balance and happiness.

Robin's narrative made me wonder how many nonbinary individuals are not receiving as much support from their families, and are not as talented, insightful, and resilient as Robin. Becoming educated about the experiences of individuals whose gender identities fall outside the man/woman dichotomy is an important first step so that we will help, and not further hurt. One cannot tell a nonbinary gender identification from the way the person looks or dresses, because they can have both male and female gender presentations. Those who do not identify with any gender have nevertheless been socialized in a binary way, as boy/girl or man/woman. Feeling comfortable asking a person how they would like to be addressed, rather than making assumptions, communicates understanding of and respect for gender diversity.

There is some confusion about what it means to be nonbinary. Some equate nonbinary with being intersex—that is, having a body not traditionally classified as male or female—but being nonbinary is not based in biology. Intersex people can be nonbinary, but so can people who are not intersex. Others equate being nonbinary with being transgender, identifying with a gender other than the one they were assigned at birth. Some nonbinary people feel this definition applies to them, but others do not.

While it may seem that the increased visibility of gender-variant individuals is a more recent phenomenon, this is not accurate: people who do not identify with the gender they have been assigned at birth have been working for centuries to fight for recognition and acceptance. Colonialism all over the world has stifled gender variance. In the United States, the Navajo Nation has long recognized four genders that roughly correlate with cisgender and transgender men and women, and they use different terms for those who "transform" into femininity and for those who "transform" into masculinity. The Mojave people describe similar identities. And the Lakota tribe believes the *winkte* people among them have supernatural powers like India's hijras. The two-spirit community is experiencing a renaissance of activism lately, but this is not a recent phenomenon. We'wha was a famous Lhamana (i.e., two-spirit) member of the Zuni tribe and may have been the first out-of-the-closet gender variant person to meet a US president when introduced to Grover Cleveland in 1886 (Brandman, 2021).

Since analysts and therapists will inevitably meet patients of different genders in their practices, we all want to examine our countertransference feelings, and approach gender-variant patients with an open mind, empathy, and sensitivity. There is some controversy among psychoanalysts about whether one should accept and affirm a patient's declared gender, given that one's gender identity is influenced by unconscious factors. This discussion mirrors the decades-long discussion in psychoanalysis about whether the analyst should affirm and validate a patient's past trauma. It was feared that doing so would limit the patient's thinking and fantasies about themselves and even contribute to implanting false memories. However, clinicians who have specialized in psychoanalytic trauma treatment have taught us that the validation of the psychic impact of trauma is essential to a patient's recovery.

As we have come to understand from Robin's autobiography, the psychological experience of not fitting in with conventional gender norms is deeply distressing and furthers the development of shameful fantasies about the self. It is incumbent upon us to fully embrace gender fluidity and suspend our judgments of a patient's gender identification. Our task as analysts is to listen and to follow the patient, and to open up the therapeutic space so that everything can be talked about. If the patient feels unconditionally accepted by their therapist/analyst, and the clinician conveys that they are not anxious about or judgmental of the patient's declared gender, patients will feel free to examine their own anxieties and conflicts, including their unconscious ones. I recommend an analytic attitude characterized by a welcoming and neutral-positive stance. As our society becomes more open, tolerant, and less gender-focused, there will be fewer patients who suffer from painful guilt and shame about not fitting in because the gender they were assigned at birth does not fit their self-experience. When we accept our patients as they are and affirm their declared gender identities, our profession will make an important contribution to alleviate gender-related suffering.

## Reference

Brandman, M. (2021). *We'wha*. National Women's History Museum, https://www.womenshistory.org/education-resources/biographies/wewha

# CHAPTER FOUR

# Nonbinary think piece

*Francesca Ely-Spence*

A couple of weeks ago, I was listening to a conversation between Brené Brown and Glennon Doyle on Brené's podcast, *Unlocking Us*. The two were talking about what it means to be a woman in today's society: What is asked of women, what is expected of women, and what is off-limits to women. Glennon was talking about her previous life, when she was still married to her husband, and she recalled a constant, unbidden question in her mind: "But wasn't it supposed to be more beautiful than this?"

I felt that question reverberate through my soul. It is something I have asked myself many times, as I believe many AFAB (assigned female at birth) people have—in relationships, in jobs, in considering the state of my life and the world generally—but it wasn't until a couple of years ago that the question began to prod at my gender identity.

Prior to 2019, if you had asked me, "How's your gender identity feeling to you? Is it still serving you?" I would have given a resounding affirmative: "Of course! I love being a woman and I love women!" And I still do love and cherish womanhood. I went to a women's college, and the sense of community, care, and encouragement that I experienced there formed tethers between myself and the legacy of womanhood that will not soon fray. However, when I left college and entered the so-called real world, I found that the identity of "woman" to which I felt so connected and the identity of "woman" that existed outside the walls of my school were wholly different. The category of "woman" was so expansive within my college that I never felt restricted, misunderstood, or invisible when I used that term to describe myself. "Woman" could hold all the parts of my identity because its definition was never limited for me. It helped that many students at my college were genderqueer themselves, which necessarily molded the culture of the school into one that openly supported gender exploration and variance (at least at the student level). However, once I began navigating the outside world as a "woman," I ran smack into a whole set of expectations, rules, and boundaries that demanded that my identity serve others, not myself. As Brené and Glennon noted, the best thing a woman can be is selfless—that is, lacking a self.

Of course, the world's notion of "woman" was something I had subscribed to in high school, when I was vaguely aware of my queerness but it was relegated to the fringes of my consciousness. I don't think I was particularly uncomfortable with a queer identity—it just wasn't relevant to me yet. I was in a healthy heterosexual relationship, and there were approximately four gay people out at my high school, so there wasn't much room for experimentation. College induced the almost painfully rapid expansion of my understanding of myself and the world, and I am forever grateful to my degrees in sociology and in women's, gender, and sexuality studies for preparing me for what was to come.

After college, I moved out to the Bay Area, and within a couple of months, I knew something was wrong. I made myself small anytime I saw someone looking at me on public transportation; I cringed when dates told me what a "pretty girl" I was; I hated looking at my body in any reflection, reeling with disgust when I did because I knew how the world perceived me and knew, with equal confidence, that what they were seeing was not me. But I didn't know "me" anymore.

I was fortunate enough to have found a supportive queer community after moving, and many of my closest friends were experimenting with their own identities at the time, trying different names, styles of presentation, and pronouns to see what felt good. I watched their processes, still not quite believing my own desire to jump in and join them, especially when I had never, not once, questioned my gender identity up to that point. One day, someone referred to me as "she," and my brain froze—who are they talking about? It happened so quickly. I just didn't connect with she/her/hers pronouns anymore. So, I tried something different: I asked my friends to start using they/them/theirs to refer to me, and they happily (almost gleefully) obliged, welcoming me into another beautiful community both like and unlike the one I had bonded with in college.

There are still parts of womanhood that serve and resonate with me, and I have brought those along with me as I continue my self-excavation, tucked like gems into the lining of myself and gleaming through the varied ways I move through the world. These do not negate my nonbinary identity. There are parts of womanhood that do not serve me, or no longer do, and I have left (or am in the process of leaving) those behind, along with the identity title of "woman." Not everyone who lets go of certain parts of an identity also lets go of that identity title. That was my choice, for myself, because it felt good to me. Glennon and Brené, even while pointing out the gaslighting and trauma and power struggles associated with the world's view of "woman," still speak of their identities as women with great tenderness, reverence, and love. All of these experiences and choices are valid as we try our best to do what makes us feel good, known, and unfettered in the world and to leave behind what we know cannot help us get free.

There is a narrative in the queer community, in terms of gender and sexuality alike, that we were all "born this way" and that we cannot change who we are. This narrative works for a lot of people; it does not work for me. I did not always "feel" nonbinary or uncomfortable with the identity of "woman." It took time, experience, learning, and growth for me to arrive here, and I don't expect my identity to now remain stagnant for the rest of my life. I expect change, and I hope that I have assembled the tools for introspection in such a way that, if I should feel that discomfort I felt in 2019 again, I can, this time, get curious about it, without self-judgment, and move away from whatever is no longer serving me and toward what resonates. In Glennon's words, "Maybe our imagination is not where we go to escape reality. Maybe our imagination is where we go to discover the truest reality that we were meant to bring into the world."

I find a nonbinary identity to be one of the purest examples of this point because a nonbinary identity can literally look and feel like anything to anyone. It is a DIY project, an ongoing construction of a personalized way of being that exists solely because it feels good to the individual. There is no gatekeeping; anyone can be nonbinary, and all you have to do is feel like you are. There are, ideally, no expectations of androgyny from nonbinary people. "Nonbinary" is not a third gender. It is a release, it is freedom of expression, it is work, it is discovery and acceptance and peace with all of the nuanced and limitless parts of ourselves.

# CHAPTER FIVE

# Thoughts by the parents of a nonbinary individual

*Harry Spence and Robin Ely*

O ur child, Francesca, was born AFAB (assigned female at birth) some twenty-five years ago. Today, they identify as nonbinary and use they/them pronouns. This is an account of our journey as parents with our child's transition from an identity gendered as female to a nongendered identity.

We start with a bit of background on Francesca's upbringing, as we think it gives some context for understanding who they are today. Francesca attended a charter school in Boston through the fifth grade, the only child from an upper-middle-class family in a class of poor or working-class children, the majority of whom were black and brown. The school ended in the fifth grade, when she[1]

---

[1] We use she/her pronouns for Francesca in this essay to describe the period of life in which they used those pronouns. For the period after their transition to they/them pronouns, we use those pronouns to apply to them in this essay.

transitioned to sixth grade at Milton Academy, a private school whose day program had started in kindergarten and continued through high school, with boarding students joining the school in the ninth grade. The transition to private school was extremely challenging academically, as we anticipated. However, we were caught off guard to find that the social transition was extremely difficult as well. Francesca had spent her elementary years almost entirely among the children of poor and working-class families, not only at school, but at home in the South End of Boston. The social environment of an elite, overwhelmingly white private school proved bewildering for Francesca, and her middle school years were extremely disorienting and lonely.

Eventually, Francesca joined three other girls in a band, with Francesca serving as the vocalist. The members of the band became fast friends, and Francesca grew ever more comfortable and successful both academically and socially through her high school years. She loved team sports but didn't particularly excel at athletics until she chose to be a goalie in both field and ice hockey, roles she loved and in which she proved very capable. In the last two years of high school, she also formed a strong romantic attachment with a boy a year ahead her, an outstanding athlete given to intellectual reflection. As parents, we were delighted to watch Francesca insist with her boyfriend that he treat her with respect and ignore the male social pressures he was subject to, and the two formed a deep, caring, and mutually respectful relationship.

We were typically indulgent liberal parents, never presuming that her sexual identity was indelibly heterosexual, and tolerant of her mild drug experimentation, so long as the circumstances assured her safety. We were supportive of her sexual relationship, and she was always open with us about her life, love and otherwise.

The transition to college allowed Francesca to shed whatever remnants of her difficult middle school years might have remained in her high school identity. On her initiative, the romantic relationship with her boyfriend ended (they have remained good friends ever since) so that she might feel entirely free to shape her identity and life in college. She attended Barnard College and immersed herself deeply in the political culture of the college, which was extremely progressive politically and socially. She played ice hockey throughout college and loved being the team's goalie. She flourished in college and formed lasting attachments with her friends there. Like many of her classmates, she began to define her sexual identity as queer. That seemed an embracing term, and we were untroubled by it.

Francesca was anxious to spread her wings after college and got a job in a tech company in San Francisco. She got her driver's license and bought a car and ticked off a checklist of new adult behaviors: getting insurance and checking accounts, starting to save money, managing her medical care. We were impressed and pleased by her independence, though not unaware of the emotional ups and downs of her life as an emerging adult.

In the spring of 2019, we visited her, and she told us she had decided to return to Boston in the summer, having grown bored and restless with her job and progressively less enamored of West Coast living, where people, she said, "worked hard to appear laid back but were just as stressed out as people on the East Coast." She preferred the lack of pretense on the East Coast. We were thrilled at the prospect of having her closer to home!

During that visit, Francesca shared her growing reflections about gender and told us that she had decided to try on an identity as asexual. This identity, she explained, relieved her of the pressure she often felt to meet others' expectations about sex and made it easier for her to simply say no when she wanted to.

A short while later, Francesca informed us that they had started using they/them pronouns and asked us to do the same when referring to them.

It seems relevant here to say that Francesca is quite strikingly beautiful—we are their parents, but that is an objective judgment. In college, they had sometimes played with and showcased their beauty, enjoying getting dressed up and taking glamorous model-style photos of themself. But Francesca did not depend on their beauty for their core identity. While they took pleasure in it, it was not something they relied on consciously for power or privilege.

Nonetheless, Francesca described how in college in New York, they would get on a subway and be aware of, but unfazed by, men looking at them. Now they were troubled by how they felt compelled to comply with the identity of "beautiful woman," even in the eyes of complete strangers. They wanted to resist the tyranny of "the male gaze" and experiment with redefining their identity as nonbinary.

We understood the desire to resist that tyranny, but we were surprised and, admittedly, a bit taken aback by their claiming of a nonbinary identity. Nevertheless, we could see that it was an excellent time in their life to undertake such a journey of discovery, and we very much respected the decisions at which they had arrived. We would do our best to comply with their request to change the pronouns we used for them.

We were curious how this experiment would unfold. We wondered, privately, of course, whether it was a phase or would prove more lasting. Interestingly, it was comforting to us that the experiment did not seem to reflect discomfort with female aspects of their identity nor did it seem to repudiate their femininity. Rather, it seemed clearly directed at reducing the power of "the male gaze." Positively, it seemed to entail expanding beyond the confines of traditional female identity to embrace a larger identity, and to test whether nonbinary pronouns enhanced their capacity to explore more ways of being in the world.

They moved back to Boston and got employment as a research assistant to Harvard faculty. Meanwhile, they indicated that the experiment with a nonbinary identity was growing more central to their identity and expressed frustration at our faltering attempts to remember their pronouns. We kept asking for forgiveness, repeatedly explaining that language habits die hard, not to mention the grammatical stumbling block of using "they" as a referent to the singular.

They were hearing nothing of it and soon, in sheer exasperation with us, told us they needed to cut off contact with us, so upsetting it was that we did not appear to be taking them seriously or trying hard enough. The rift was painful; they didn't communicate with us for a month. While we respected their need for distance, we were hurt and felt confused. The break ended with a session the three of us had with Francesca's therapist. In that session, it became clear to us that what Francesca most wanted and needed was for us to simply affirm and validate them, to "see" and accept them fully. We got that. And once we got that, we were able to work through our own issues (see "Robin's perspective" below) and to provide—with ease—the validation and affirmation they had been seeking.

As the months of the pandemic have passed, Francesca has changed their self-presentation, with a wardrobe that is much less traditionally feminine. Nonetheless, they continue to take pleasure in playing with their appearance, bleaching their short hair and on occasion using modest amounts of makeup. We still struggle a bit with pronouns, but we correct each other. We seem to have settled into the new situation comfortably, but our comfort derives in part from what Francesca's nonbinary identity is not: it is not a repudiation of the feminine nor a wish to transition to a male identity, but rather an exploration of all the things that they can be between and beyond those two axes to which most of the rest of us have constrained ourselves. They do not seem in any way to be in pain over issues of identity, but instead seem to us to be happy in their nonbinary identity. They are clear that they believe that the world would be a better place if gender were not a central definition of identity, and they call us out when we look reflexively to know someone's gender as the primary aspect of their identity. We count ourselves probably too old to expect to alter that reflex in this lifetime, but we are sympathetic to the urge to diminish, even abolish it.

We are very much intrigued with Francesca's explorations. We obviously wonder how they will continue to unfold, but we are immensely proud of the person that Francesca is proving to be. Certainly, the rejection of gender as a defining category of human identity is a huge insurgency, and we look to find unacknowledged resistances or anxieties in our reactions. We are comforted that Francesca's gender explorations do not seem grounded in a deep sense of dissatisfaction with their historic gender identity, but rather are grounded in the cultural constraints that gender identity so easily imposes. We understand Francesca's nonbinary identity to be an exploration and expression of freedom, and we applaud it.

## Robin Ely's added perspective

While the account above is accurate from my perspective, I feel there is more to the story of my experience parenting a child who, assigned female at birth, has taken an identity as gender nonbinary. If I am honest, as much as I have supported Francesca and been proud of their insistence on living their truth—no matter how inconvenient to them or to others—I will admit to having had some difficulty with their decision to adopt they/them pronouns. And my difficulty was not just because language habits die hard or because "they" as a referent to the singular had always been ungrammatical. Even more disconcerting to both Francesca and me, I eventually came to see, was that I was having trouble letting go of Francesca's gender identity as a woman—an identity that, to that point, we had shared, and that shared experience had been a great source of joy for me.

I had very much wanted to have a girl. I was thrilled when the doctor read the sonogram during my amniocentesis and announced that we were having "a little princess" (exact words). I reveled in Francesca's femininity. We did "mother–daughter" things together: went shopping, had tea at the Plaza (where Eloise lived!), saw *Wicked*, watched chick flicks and *Grey's Anatomy*, swooning together over the cute bad-boy doctor, and generally felt a mutual identification through our shared gender identity.

But I am also a feminist—have spent my career as a feminist scholar of gender and race relations in organizations—and I very much wanted to equip Francesca to resist gender oppression.

So I was ambivalent. On the one hand, I feared that Francesca's claiming of a gender nonbinary identity would mean a loss of connection; on the other hand, I was also so proud of them, knowing their own mind, bucking the sexist system that defined them in ways they found oppressive.

And so, we struggled for a while—the period leading up to the month-long break in our communication. I used the wrong pronouns routinely; they were exasperated; I wanted forgiveness; they wanted validation. We ping-ponged like that, rather painfully, for several weeks.

But ever since those tough middle-school years, Francesca has proved to have a remarkable capacity to access and share their feelings—and to insist that we listen. Their insistence has made me a better parent. So, true to form, when it was clear that I wasn't fully "getting it," they didn't relent. The turning point for me came in the therapy session we mentioned above, when I finally was able to see that my job was to listen and affirm, and when I made a mistake with the pronouns, to simply correct myself and move on, not to defend or explain myself. That opened the way for me to be able to share my feelings and for them to listen and affirm.

I've learned that Francesca and I don't need a shared gender identity to be close—we are perhaps closer now than ever before. I am bursting with admiration for their courage to defy the gender binary and to claim instead identities that feel right to them, regardless of the inconvenience of their choices to a world that wants to pigeon-hole and objectify their beauty. (I am also grateful that they still let me call them, in private, my "baby girl"— we've discussed it, and, for both of us, that term is one more of endearment than of a gendered identity.) As a gender scholar, I am grateful that they are stretching my mind in ways probably nothing—and no one—else could. As their mother, I find comfort in the knowledge that they know their mind and won't bend to convention simply to fit in. They are a role model for me in their unwavering capacity to remain true to their experience, to insist on speaking their truth.

# CHAPTER SIX

# Some recent thoughts on gender

*Malkah T. Notman*

W hen Robert Stoller introduced the concept of gender as different from anatomical sex, there was a good deal of discussion about the implications of this idea. The concept of gender role, reflecting conventional expectations about the behavior and interests of males and females, also received a lot of attention. For those of us who were women in medicine, this career path was seen as partly consistent with the feminine gender role of taking care of people and partly deviant, since it involved an interest in science and professional achievement. Girls wanting to be active in male sports such as baseball or boys showing interest in art coasted along the edge of conventional acceptance. In adulthood, women's and men's roles were more narrowly defined, depending on the particular culture. It seemed that some women wanting to be men were desiring the greater freedom, the possibility of expression of aggression, or participation in particular activities and roles available to men. The depreciated way in which women were regarded and the sexism in the culture also needed to be considered in understanding preferences. The question of sexual object choice, same sex or opposite sex, was another issue.

The current discussions about gender dysphoria and fluidity go beyond consideration of gender roles. There is explicit focus on and concern about the body. Some people feel they are in the wrong body. It is not always clear what they feel is wrong. This can have various component meanings, for example, the breasts can feel particularly problematic to someone who is looking for a male identity. I think we have a great deal to learn about these feelings and their relationship to someone's sense of identity.

Currently gender transition is more prevalent. I do believe that some small group of people feel uncomfortable identifying with either gender and consider themselves nonbinary. These are genuine feelings. It is important not to pathologize them as psychoanalysis used to pathologize homosexuality. They are pathologized when thought of as defensive rather than genuine.

We need to understand more about the role of development, of biology, of identification with parents, of genetic "givens" and how they unfold. Daniel Jacobs describes these topics in more detail.

I have also become interested in another aspect of the trans experience: how considerations of fertility and reproductive possibility enter these choices.

Female bodies have the organs necessary for reproduction. Not every girl or woman wants to have children. It is, however, part of the ego ideal and unconscious or conscious body concept of most girls and women that pregnancy and childbirth are possible. I have not been aware that the issue of fertility, the possibility of pregnancy, is a major discussion point in the consideration of trans choices, feelings, decisions. Do those females changing to males consciously think about giving up the possibility of child-bearing with regret or with relief? Is it a wish or a concern for males transitioning to females? Having spent many years studying aspects of pregnancy, fertility, and abortion, I am interested in how these issues fit together. It would be interesting to explore them psychoanalytically.

I am also concerned about another component of the current atmosphere, which has encouraged and supported medical as well as surgical procedures in adolescents. We know that the brain does not completely mature until an individual's twenties, so some of these gender feelings may reflect more transient issues, and may change with further maturation. I think this may be particularly true with feelings about fertility. We know that the wish to have a child can develop relatively late in some women. They can be at the edge of their fertile periods. Many women then look into fertility programs. It would be important to know more about how a person thinking of gender change imagines the future and what that holds. How one visualizes the future in a different identity than one used to as a child would be important to understand.

Obviously, this applies to many more issues than gender—it includes social conditions and expectations. It is important to know how each gender fits into a particular culture. How do one's predictions hold up?

There is a great deal that psychoanalysis can contribute to this complicated and fascinating topic.

# CHAPTER SEVEN

# Reflections on sexuality and gender

*Daniel Jacobs*

> *I cannot discover myself until I have a chance to be myself.*
> —James Merrill, poet

> *If Dora lived today, she would be gender fluid.*
> —Anonymous

The remarkable and moving contributions of Robin Haas and Francesca Ely-Spence are accounts of lived experience, both painful and joyful, depicting in the most personal terms the search for an authentic expression of self. These vivid experiences are coupled with Shari Thurer's history of misunderstanding and discrimination that still persist in our country and profession. The contributions of Francesca's parents, Robin Ely and the late Harry Spence, tell the tale of many parents who are surprised by their children's gender fluidity and struggle to understand it. They illustrate how parents can educate themselves (with their children's help) as to who their offspring are not and who they thought or hoped they were (Rahilly, 2015). Francesca's sense of themself changes over time, evidence that gender is a lifelong unfolding rather than set at a moment in time (Ehrensaft, 2014). Harry and Robin successfully, but not without struggle, change with them. As a result, the bonds of love between parent and child are sustained.

Rita Teusch's contributions underline the necessity of genderfluid individuals to be heard and respected. She notes:

> The psychological experience of not fitting in with conventional gender norms is deeply distressing and furthers the development of shameful fantasies about the self. It is incumbent upon us [as analysts] to fully embrace gender fluidity and suspend our judgments of a patient's gender identity.

This necessary embrace does not preclude questions concerning the nature of human development. Yet, for some, even thinking about influences on the formation of gender identity is perceived as a hostile act (Bell, 2020). The questions I am about to ask are not concerned with judging any particular gender identity, but an attempt to further understand the biological, psychological, and cultural contributions to its formation. To what extent, for instance, is gender identity influenced by genetic makeup (Leinung & Wu, 2017), or by particular *in utero* conditions? (Belluck, 2019). What are the roles, if any, of sibling order and sibling anatomy in determining feeling about one's sexual self? What is the influence of conscious or unconscious hostile and/or loving feelings toward a parent? How might infantile or adolescent trauma affect the sense of gendered self? How does a child, once aware of sexual difference, explain it? How might these infantile explanations (often repressed) affect gender identity? (Galenson et al., 1975). What role does the educational environment play in allowing the expression of sexual diversity? Malkah Notman, in her essay, inquires about the interface of procreativity and gender choice. These questions are not asked with the intention of rooting out pathology, but only to try to deepen understanding of our human condition.

In the past, those who are not heterosexual have often been wary of seeking psychotherapy. They fear their sexual identity and object choice will be challenged, pathologized, and judged. People of color feel they will be doubly misjudged. LGBTQ persons of any race demand respect for their self-definition, before any exploration of the problems for which they seek help can begin. They have reasons to be concerned about seeking treatment. As Thurer points out in her essay, until recently most members of the American Psychoanalytic Association, influenced by the medicalization of psychoanalysis with its emphasis on pathology and cure, thought of

> ... two complementary genders, each of which had an appropriate role and distinctive proclivities [ergo gender dichotomy]—in poet Adrienne Rich's words "compulsory heterosexuality." The myopia of this view might not have been so damaging had parochial midcentury psychoanalytic thinking held less sway over the collective imagination. At that time, it powerfully influenced social science, education, child-rearing practices, and the law ... and the very formation of psychiatric diagnostic categories. With its enormous prestige, it served to define what was healthy, good and right; and deviant sexuality, and certainly "deviant" gender identity, did not qualify.

Indeed, queer inclinations were considered pathological, and in the decades that followed these ideas hardened.

I was subject to this way of thinking as a psychiatric resident.

Every week, illustrious members of the New York Psychoanalytic Society and Institute (Walter Stewart, Andrew Peto, Martin Wangh, Edith Jacobson, and other luminaries) arrived at Jacobi Hospital to conduct seminars. Among them was Dr. Charles Socarides. He was a midsized, solidly built man with a shock of thick dark hair who fought defiantly against giving ground. He was in his mid-forties then, not yet four-times married; not yet founder of the National Association for Research and Therapy of Homosexuality (NARTH)—a national organization that still promotes "conversion therapy"; not yet seeing his son, Richard, become an avid gay rights advocate (Socarides, R., 2013).

Dr. Socarides' voice was clear, forceful, deliberate, and brooked no interruption. He was intelligent and articulate—an expert we listened to with both awe and discomfort. We were being taught by being told. Socarides postulated that homosexuality was a mental illness that could be treated by psychoanalysis. He told us male homosexuality typically develops in the first two years of life, during the boy's pre-Oedipal stage of development. In his view, a controlling mother prevents her son from separating from her, while a weak or rejecting father does not support the boy's efforts to escape from the maternal dyad. He held that homosexuality was a transitional condition somewhere between psychosis, borderline states, and/or the neuroses. He believed that the analyst who treats a homosexual must have (consciously or unconsciously) arrived at a diagnostic conclusion that the existence of an intrapsychic heterosexual solution is possible and that the patient can use the analytic method in its attainment (Socarides, C. W., 1962). Many analysts agreed. The possibility that some of the conflicts and suffering of their homosexual patients had to do with the way they were viewed by society did not enter the discussion. Furthermore, the emphasis on pre-Oedipal problems and the dangers of regression to psychosis gave impetus to the feeling that many homosexuals could not be analyzed or become analysts themselves unless they were able to change their sexual orientation (Socarides, C. W., 1962, 1969, 1970).

All of this was delivered with such certainty that it was hard to think otherwise: Homosexuality was a maladaptive solution to intrapsychic conflict and to difficulties in separation. Effective treatment meant change of sexual orientation. There was little thought given to how the patient's acceptance of and accommodation to the analyst's formulations might in itself be a sexually displaced enactment. Or that persecution was making the patient unhappy, not their sexual orientation. Freud's (1935) letter to a mother in which he states that homosexuality is "nothing to be ashamed of, no vice, no degradation; it cannot be classified as an illness" was forgotten.

Dr. Socarides gave many clinical examples of his work. He claimed "success" in conversion in about 40% of those homosexuals he treated. He offered no room for alternative points of view and, if any of us had them, we were loath to take on "the expert" or to state them to one another. Some of us wanted to be analysts. None of us wanted to be singled out by Socarides or anyone else as being mentally ill.

In those days, the word "queer" was a pejorative used to describe a homosexual. Gender fluidity was equated with bisexuality and having a "polymorphous perverse" mental state. So it is understandable that many LGBTQ and nonbinary individuals now fear being misunderstood and pathologized by psychiatrists just as homosexuals were in the past and, in some instances, still are. There are still debates about bathroom use (Levin, 2019) and the practice of sport teams (Graham, 2021) to categorize and exclude people whose gender is different than expected. Even those therapists who feel they are "neutral and open" may not be so (Nardone, 2018). They may not be sufficiently aware that treatments are determined by the dynamics of how "each of us lives in our particular culture and how, in turn, that culture lives, for better or worse, within us" (Holmes, 2021, p. 256; Bell, 2020).

These concerns about being misunderstood have led many to seek therapists whose lived experience matches their own. Gay men often seek a gay male therapist. Many trans college students prefer to see a trans therapist (of whom there are not enough). Women often request a female therapist, and many people of color choose to talk to someone who is not "white." These preferences are very understandable and are, at the same time, somewhat lamentable. They suggest that we cannot really understand or talk intimately with another whose background and experience is different from ours. This view not only limits choice, but suggests that imagination, empathy, and compassion cannot sufficiently cross physical and cultural boundaries: that we can only talk openly with our "own kind." If taken to extremes, this view leads to drawing rigid boundaries between those who are acceptable and those who are not. It denies us a common humanity and the empathic capacity to put ourselves in another's shoes. For us to trust one another outside very limited boundaries requires what Hart (2019) terms "radical openness." This is the capacity (on the part of both patient and therapist) to notice, question, and relinquish presumptions about the self and the other.

If there are dangers in rigid distinctions, the opposite may also be true. Some psychoanalytic institutes, I believe, have made an unfortunate decision. They no longer require candidates in analytic training to analyze at least one patient born with a penis and one with a vagina. From birth, we live in bodies with specific sexual equipment and gonads, like them or not, wanting to change them or not. Understanding what psychically it means to start in a "boy body" or a "girl body" is important. Candidates need the experience of learning how children born with different sexual apparatuses first experienced their bodies and how they develop fantasies that originated in the discovery of initial differences.

I have not even touched upon the thorny questions around alteration of the body, a subject taken up more extensively by contributors to *The Psychoanalytic Study of the Child* (2014). At what age is an individual mature enough to make a decision that seriously, and perhaps permanently, changes their anatomy either through hormones or surgery? Knight (2014) raises questions about the psychological cost of premature closure, of a child not entering puberty and not experiencing the natural development of the body. She believes it is important for children to experience "the expectable disequilibrium of self structures that gives [them] the chance to play with different possibilities of gender role identity" (p. 61). She writes that children have neither the legal right nor the mature judgment to make such life-changing decisions. They must rely on their parents and adults who may not be sufficiently knowledgeable of issues in child development. Children may feel pressure to be or do what those grown-ups (consciously or unconsciously) want and so retain their love. There is some evidence, furthermore, that most gender variance in children does not persist into adolescence (Butler & Hutchinson, 2020). There is no way to reliably identify which prepubertal child, as puberty and adolescence proceeds, will persist in wanting to change sexes (deVries et al., 2014). All the more reason for therapists to remain well trained and curious, but non-judgmental, allowing children to explore as many of the influences upon them as possible (Bell, 2020).

So, when and for whom is it appropriate to chemically delay puberty? (Ehrensaft, 2014). De Vries et al. (2011) report that for transgender children, behavioral and emotional problems as well as depressive symptoms are decreased with hormonal puberty blockers (though they include no control group). Children who *persist* in their transgender preference into adolescence are more likely to continue this tendency into adult life (Zucker 2008). For them, post-pubertal sex-altering surgery is a more complicated and potentially a more traumatic procedure. Yet, when does a patient's belief in changing their gender or anatomy mask problems of relating and loving that such medical interventions cannot solve (Withers, 2020)?

There are no clear answers yet to these questions; no response will be appropriate for all individuals. But questions must continue to be raised. We must also be aware of how the subject of delay of puberty as well as gender-changing surgery can be politicized, like gender choice itself, and move away from these tougher questions.

So where do we go from here? Hopefully, to continue to listen and learn from our patients; to foster further discussion about gender diversity, to increase our understanding by judicious reading like that suggested by psychologist Oren Gozlan in the following chapter in this book. Saketopoulou (2020) puts the matter clearly: "Trans has revealed psychoanalysis to have been woefully unprepared to think about gender beyond the perception of sexual difference. We are in uncharted territory. Knowledge will build slowly" (p. 1028).

This book enters that new and unmapped landscape. Its goals are modest. They are to tell a history, to share experiences, and to invite further exploration of gender identity and sexual choice. Join us in that journey.

## References

Bell, D. (2020). First, do no harm. *International Journal of Psychoanalysis, 101*, 1031–1038. https://doi.org/10.1080/00207578.2020.1810885

Belluck, P. (2019, August 29). Many genes influence same-sex sexuality, not a single "gay gene". *New York Times.* https://www.nytimes.com/2019/08/29/science/gay-gene-sex.html

Butler, C., & Hutchinson, A. (2020). Debate: The pressing need for research and services for gender desisters/detransitioners. *Child and Adolescent Mental Health, 25*(1), 45–47. https://doi.org/10.1111/camh.12361

de Vries, A. L., McGuire, J. K., Steensma, T. D., Wagenaar, E. C., Doreleijers, T. A., & Cohen-Kettenis, P. T. (2014). Young adult psychological outcome after puberty suppression and gender reassignment. *Pediatrics, 134*(4), 696–704. https://doi.org/10.1542/peds.2013–2958

de Vries, A. L., Steensma, T. D., Doreleijers, T. A., & Cohen-Kettenis, P. T. (2011). Puberty suppression in adolescents with gender identity disorder: a prospective follow-up study. *The Journal of Sexual Medicine, 8*(8), 2276–2283. https://doi.org/10.1111/j.1743-6109.2010.01943.x

Ehrensaft, D. (2014). Listening and learning from gender-nonconforming children. *Psychoanalytic Study of the Child, 68*(1), 28–56. DOI: 10.1080/00797308.2015.11785504

Freud, S. (1935, April 9). Letter from Sigmund Freud to Anonymous. *Letters of Sigmund Freud 1873–1939, 51*, 423–424.

Galenson, E., Vogel, S., Blau, S., & Roiphe, H. (1975). Disturbance in sexual identity beginning at 18 months of age. *International Review of Psychoanalysis, 2*, 389–397.

Gozlan, O. (2022). Transsexuality bibliography. In Thurer, S. (Ed.), *Beyond the Binary: Essays on Gender* (pp. 87–99). Bicester, UK: Phoenix.

Graham, R. (2021, August 11). The lasting impact of LGBTQ athletes at the Tokyo Olympics. *The Boston Globe.* https://www.bostonglobe.com/2021/08/10/opinion/lasting-impact-lgbtq-athletes-tokyo-olympics/

Hart, A. (2019). The discriminatory gesture: A psychoanalytic consideration of posttraumatic reactions to incidents of racial discrimination. *Psychoanalytic Social Work, 26*(1), 5–24. https://doi.org/10.1080/15228878.2019.1604241

Holmes, D. E. (2021). "I do not have a racist bone in my body": Psychoanalytic perspectives on what is lost and not mourned in our culture's persistent racism. *Journal of the American Psychoanalytic Association, 69*(2), 237–258. https://doi.org/10.1177/00030651211009518

Knight, R. (2014). Free to be you and me: Normal gender-role fluidity—commentary on Diane Ehrensaft's "Listening and learning from gender-nonconforming children." *The Psychoanalytic Study*

*of the Child, 68*(1), 57–70. https://doi.org/10.1080/00797308.201
5.11785505

Leinung, M., & Wu, C. (2017). The biologic basis of transgender identity: 2D:4D finger length ratios implicate a role for prenatal androgen activity. *Endocrine Practice, 23*(6), 669–671. https://doi.org/10.4158/
EP161528.OR

Levin, D. (2019, July 23). North Carolina reaches settlement on "bathroom bill". *New York Times.* https://www.nytimes.com/2019/07/23/
us/north-carolina-transgender-bathrooms.html

Merrill, J. (1993). *A Different Person: A Memoir.* New York, NY: Knopf.

Nardone, M. (2018). The powerful and covert role of culture in gender discrimination and inequality. *Contemporary Psychoanalysis, 54*(4), 747–762. https://doi.org/10.1080/00107530.2018.1540258

Rahilly, E. P. (2015). The gender binary meets the gender-variant child: Parents' negotiations with childhood gender variance. *Gender & Society, 29*(3), 338–361. https://doi.org/10.1177/0891243214563069

Saketopoulou, A. (2020). Thinking psychoanalytically, thinking better: Reflections on transgender. *The International Journal of Psychoanalysis, 101*(5), 1019–1030. https://doi.org/10.1080/00207578.2020.1810884

Socarides, C. W. (1962). Theoretical and clinical aspects of overt female homosexuality. *Journal of the American Psychoanalytic Association, 10*(3), 579–592. https://doi.org/10.1177/000306516201000307

Socarides, C. W. (1969). Psychoanalytic therapy of a male homosexual. *The Psychoanalytic Quarterly, 38*(2), 173–190. https://doi.org/10.
1080/21674086.1969.11926487

Socarides, C. W. (1970). A psychoanalytic study of the desire for sexual transformation ('transsexualism'): The plaster-of-Paris man. *The International Journal of Psycho-Analysis, 51*(3), 341–349.

Socarides, R. (2013, April 8). Coming out to my father. *The New Yorker.* https://www.newyorker.com/news/news-desk/coming-out-to-
my-father

Withers, R. (2020). Transgender medicalization and the attempt to evade psychological distress. *The Journal of Analytical Psychology*, 65(5), 865–889. https://doi.org/10.1111/1468-5922.12641

Zucker, K. J. (2008). On the "natural history" of gender identity disorder in children. *Journal of the American Academy of Child and Adolescent Psychiatry*, 47(12), 1361–1363. https://doi.org/10.1097/CHI.0b013e31818960cf

# CHAPTER EIGHT

# Transsexuality bibliography

*Oren Gozlan*

The field of transsexual studies has itself been transitioning in recent decades, and the very notion of transitioning is no longer conceptualized within the binary of "either/or." Recent transsexual discourses destabilize the invisible ideology of sexual difference and its definition in social, political, and psychoanalytic discourses, putting into question the notion of gender itself. The emancipatory potential of new understandings of transsexuality has yet to be actualized. Essentialist tropes of origin continue to stubbornly permeate within and outside of the psychanalytic field. The bibliography I selected offers an entrance into contemporary theories of transsexuality, their cleavages and contradictions, as well as into the constellation of fantasies concerning gender and sexuality circulating in the psychoanalytic field and beyond. It presents a cross-section of interdisciplinary discourses, proposing a broad view of gender and of transsexuality.

I have chosen an array of articles, books, and book chapters published mostly within the last decade; however, included are earlier writings on gender that are foundational to the field. The writings are predominantly but not exclusively psychoanalytic. Social and political discourses as well as literary, aesthetic, and philosophical perspectives are also included as a way of thinking of transsexuality as situated in culture and as subject to its social structures. Articles engage ethical, clinical, pedagogical, and epistemological dilemmas and provide a way of exploring the psychical and heuristic potential of transsexuality to engage the larger question of the relation between sexuality and identity. The present bibliography is by no means exhaustive. Yet the range of interdisciplinary articles place in tension the concept of transsexuality as an identity, as apparatus, as defense, as inheritance, as symptom and solution, and as the hypnotizing effect of objects.

## Introductory scenes

Ames, J. (Ed.) (2005). *Sexual Metamorphosis: An Anthology of Transsexual Memoirs*. New York, NY: Vintage.

Balsam, R., & Harris, A. (2012). Maternal embodiment: A conversation between Rosemary Balsam and Adrienne Harris. *Studies in Gender and Sexuality, 13*: 33–52.

Bloom, A. (2002). *Normal: Transsexual CEOs, Crossdressing Cops, and Hermaphrodites with Attitude*. New York, NY: Random House.

Bornstein, K., & Bergman, S. B. (2010). *Gender Outlaws: The Next Generation*. Berkeley, CA: Seal Press.

Boylan, J. F. (2003). *She's Not There: A Life in Two Genders*. New York, NY: Broadway.

Butler, J. (1990). *Gender Trouble*. New York, NY: Routledge.

Butler, J. (2001). Doing justice to someone: Sex reassignment and allegories of transsexuality. *GLQ: A Journal of Lesbian and Gay Studies, 7*: 621–636.

Colapinto, J. (2000). *As Nature Made Him: The Boy Who Was Raised as a Girl.* New York, NY: HarperCollins.

Diamond, M., & Sigmundson, H. K. (1997). Sex reassignment at birth: Long-term review and clinical implications. *Archives of Pediatrics and Adolescent Medicine, 151*: 298–304.

di Ceglie, D. (Ed.) (1998). *A Stranger in My Own Body: Atypical Gender Identity Development and Mental Health.* London: Karnac.

Marcus, L., Marcus, K., Yaxte, S. M., & Marcus, K. (2015). Genderqueer: One family's experience with gender variance. *Psychoanalytic. Inquiry, 35*(8): 795–808.

## Cultural conundrums

Chodorow, N. J. (1994). *Femininities, Masculinities, Sexualities: Freud and Beyond.* Lexington, KY: University Press of Kentucky.

Connell, R. (2010). Two cans of paint: A transsexual life story, with reflections on gender change and history. *Sexualities, 13*(1): 3–19.

Connell, R. (2012). Transsexual women and feminist thought: Toward new understanding and new politics. *Journal of Women in Culture and Society, 37*(4): 857–881.

Connell, R. (2021). *Gender: In World Perspective.* New York, NY: Polity.

Faludi, S. (2016). *In the Dark Room.* New York, NY: Metropolitan.

Gherovici, P., & Steinkoler, M. (Eds.) (2021). *Psychoanalysis, Gender and Sexualities: From Feminism to Trans\*.* Cambridge, UK: Cambridge University Press.

Gozlan, O. (2017). Stalled on the stall: Reflections on a strained discourse. *Transgender Studies Quarterly, 4*(3–4): 451–471.

Gozlan, O. (Ed.) (2018). *Current Critical Debates in the Field of Transsexual Studies: In Transition.* New York, NY: Routledge.

Gozlan, O. (2021). In difference: Feminism and transgender in the field of phantasy. In: P. Gherovici & M. Steinkoler (Eds.), *Psychoanalysis, Gender and Sexualities: From Feminism to Trans\*.* Cambridge, UK: Cambridge University Press.

Hinchy, J. (2020). *Governing Gender and Sexuality in Colonial India: The Hijra C. 1850–1900.* Cambridge, UK: Cambridge University Press.

Lakshmīnārāyana, T. (2015). *Me Hijra, Me Laxmi.* Oxford, UK: Oxford University Press.

Lieberman, J. (2018). *Clinical Evolutions on the Superego, Body, and Gender in Psychoanalysis.* New York, NY: Routledge.

Mesch, R. (2020). *Before Trans: Three Gender Stories from Nineteenth-Century France.* Stanford, CA: Stanford University Press.

Namaste, V. (2000). *Invisible Lives: The Erasure of Transsexual and Transgender People.* Chicago, IL: University of Chicago Press.

Rose, J. (2016). Who do you think you are? *London Review of Books, 38*(9). https://www.lrb.co.uk/the-paper/v38/n09/jacqueline-rose/who-do-you-think-you-are

Serano, J. (2007). *Whipping Girl: A Transsexual Woman on Sexism and the Scapegoating of Femininity.* Emeryville, CA: Seal Press.

Stryker, S. (2008). *Transgender History.* Berkeley, CA: Seal Press.

Valentine, D. (2007). *Imagining Transgender: An Ethnography of a Category.* Durham, NC: Duke University Press.

## Transitioning

Butler, J. (2001). Doing justice to someone: Sex reassignment and allegories of transsexuality. *GLQ: A Journal of Lesbian and Gay Studies, 7*: 621–636.

Ehrensaft, D. (2009). One pill makes you boy, one pill makes you girl. *International Journal of Applied Psychoanalytic Studies, 6*(1): 12–24.

Gherovici, P. (2010). *Please Select Your Gender: From the Invention of Hysteria to the Democratizing of Transgenderism.* New York: NY: Routledge.

Gozlan, O. (2011). Transsexual surgery: A novel reminder and a navel remainder. *International Forum of Psychoanalysis, 20*(1): 45–52.

Gozlan, O. (2015). *Transsexuality and the Art of Transitioning: A Lacanian Perspective.* New York, NY: Routledge.

Hurst, R. A. J. (2015). *Surface Imaginations: Cosmetic Surgery, Photography, and Skin*. Montreal, QC: McGill-Queen's University Press.

Lemma, A. (2012). Research off the couch: Re-visiting the transsexual conundrum. *Psychoanalytic Psychotherapy, 26*(4): 263–281.

Lemma, A. (2016). Present without past: The disruption of temporal integration in a case of transsexuality. *Psychoanalytic Inquiry, 36*(5): 360–370.

## The psychoanalytic clinic

Cavanagh, S. L. (2018). Principles for psychoanalytic work with trans clients. In: O. Gozlan (Ed.), *Current Critical Debates in the Field of Transsexual Studies: In Transition* (pp. 89–101). New York, NY: Routledge.

Evzonas, N., & Laufer, L. (2019). The therapist's transition. *Psychoanalytic Review, 106*(5): 385–416.

Hansbury, G. (2011). King Kong & Goldilocks: Imagining transmasculinities through the trans–trans dyad. *Psychoanalytic Dialogues, 21*(2): 210–220.

Hansbury, G. (2017). The masculine vaginal: Working with queer men's embodiment at the transgender edge. *Journal of the American Psychoanalytic Association, 65*(6): 1009–1031.

Pellegrini, A., & Saketopoulou, A. (2019). On taking sides: they/them pronouns, gender and the psychoanalyst. *Psychoanalysis Today.* http://www.psychoanalysis.today/en-GB/PT-Articles/Pellegrini1 67541/On-taking-sides-they-them-pronouns,-gender-and-the.aspx

Perelberg, R. J. (2018). The riddle of anxiety: Between the familiar and the unfamiliar. *International Journal of Psycho-Analysis, 99*(4): 810–827.

Quinodoz, D. (1998). A fe/male transsexual patient in psychoanalysis. *International Journal of Psycho-Analysis, 79*: 95–111.

## Children and adolescents

de Vries, A. L., & Cohen-Kettenis, P. T. (2012). Clinical management of gender dysphoria in children and adolescents: The Dutch approach. *Journal of Homosexuality, 59*(3): 301–320.

Drescher, J., & Byne, W. (2012). Gender dysphoric/gender variant (GD/GV) children and adolescents: Summarizing what we know and what we have yet to learn. *Journal of Homosexuality, 59*(3): 501–510.

Drescher, J., & Byne, W. (Eds.) (2013). *Treating Transgender Children and Adolescents: An Interdisciplinary Discussion.* New York, NY: Routledge.

Ehrensaft, D. (2011). Boys will be girls, girls will be boys: Children affect parents as parents affect children in gender nonconformity. *Psychoanalytic Psychology, 28*: 528–548.

Ehrensaft, D. (2014). Found in transition: Our littlest transgender people. *Contemporary Psychoanalysis, 50*: 571–592.

Ehrensaft, D. (2018). Realities and myths: The gender affirmative model of care for children and youth. In: O. Gozlan (Ed.), *Current Critical Debates in the Field of Transsexual Studies: In Transition* (pp. 102–114). New York, NY: Routledge.

Elliot, P. (2001). A psychoanalytic reading of transsexual embodiment. *Studies in Gender and Sexuality, 2*: 295–325.

Fast, I. (1984). *Gender Identity: A Differentiation Model.* Hillsdale, NJ: The Analytic Press.

Fast, I. (1990). Aspects of early gender development: Toward a reformulation. *Psychoanalytic Psychology, 7(Suppl)*: 105–117.

Lemma, A. (2013). The body one has and the body one is: Understanding the transsexual's need to be seen. *The International Journal of Psycho-Analysis, 94*(2): 277–292.

Saketopoulou, A. (2011a). Queer children, new objects: The place of futurity in Loewald's thinking. *Division Review, 1*: 38–39.

Saketopoulou, A. (2011b). Minding the gap: Intersections between gender, race, and class in work with gender variant children. *Psychoanalytic Dialogues, 21*(2): 192–209.

Saketopoulou, A. (2014). Mourning the body as bedrock: Developmental considerations in treating transsexual patients analytically. *Journal of the American Psychoanalytic Association, 62*(5): 773–806.

Sherer, I., Rosenthal, S. M., Ehrensaft, D., & Baum, J. (2012). Child and Adolescent Gender Center: a multidisciplinary collaboration to improve the lives of gender nonconforming children and teens. *Pediatric Revue, 33*(6): 273–275.

Suchet, M. (2011). Crossing over. *Psychoanalytic Dialogues, 21*: 172–191.

Winograd, W. (2014). The wish to be a boy: Gender dysphoria and identity confusion in a self-identified transgender adolescent. *Psychoanalytic Social Work, 21*: 55–74.

## Conceptual transformations

### Question of gender identity and identification

Barkai, A. R. (2017). Troubling gender or engendering trouble? The problem with gender dysphoria in psychoanalysis. *Psychoanalytic Review, 104*(1): 1–32.

Benjamin, J. (1996). In defense of gender ambiguity. *Gender & Psychoanalysis, 1*: 27–43.

Butler, J. (1995). Melancholy gender-refused identification. *Psychoanalytic Dialogues, 5*(2): 165–180.

Corbett, K. (1998). Cross-gendered identifications and homosexual boyhood: Toward a more complex theory of gender. *American Journal of Orthopsychiatry, 68*: 352–360.

Drescher, J. (2007). From bisexuality to intersexuality: Rethinking gender categories. *Contemporary Psychoanalysis, 43*: 204–228.

Ehrensaft, D. (2011). *Gender Born, Gender Made: Raising Healthy Gender-nonconforming Children.* New York, NY: The Experiment.

Fast, I. (1999). Aspects of core gender identity. *Psychoanalytic Dialogues, 9*(5): 633–622.

Gerdes, K. (2014). Performativity. *Transgender Studies Quarterly, 1*(1–2): 148–150.

Goldner, V. (2011). Trans: Gender in free fall. *Psychoanalytic Dialogues, 21*: 159–171.

Gozlan, O. (2011). From Freud's theory of polymorphous perversity to transsexuality: Psychoanalysis today. *Canadian Network for Psychoanalysis and Culture.* https://cnpcrcpc.com/cnpc-1-the-freudian-legacy-today-2015/

Hansbury, G. (2005). The middle men: An introduction to the transmasculine identities. *Studies in Gender and Sexuality, 6*: 241–264.

Harris, A. (1996). The conceptual power of multiplicity. *Contemporary Psychoanalysis, 32*(4): 537–552.

Harris, A. (2011). Gender as a strange attractor: Discussion of the transgender symposium. *Psychoanalytic Dialogues, 21*(2): 230–238.

Hughs, L. (2018). Wronging the right-body narrative: On the universality of gender uncertainty. In: O. Gozlan (Ed.), *Current Critical Debates in the Field of Transsexual Studies; In Transition* (pp. 181–193). New York, NY: Routledge.

Lemma, A. (2018). Trans-itory identities: Some psychoanalytic reflections on transgender identities. *International Journal of Psycho-Analysis, 99*(5): 1089–1106.

Lemma, A. (2019). Trans-itorische identitäten: Einige psychoanalytische Überlegungen zu transgender-identitäten. *Internationale Psychoanalyse, 14*: 225–250.

Pula, J. (2015). Understanding gender through the lens of transgender experience. *Psychoanalytic Inquiry, 35*(8): 809–822.

Stoller, R. (1968). *Sex and Gender: The Transsexual Experiment.* London, UK: Hogarth.

Stoller, R. (1979). A contribution to the study of gender identity: Follow-up. *International Journal of Psycho-Analysis, 60*: 433–441.

Sullivan, N. (2006). Transmogrification (un)becoming other(s). In: S. Stryker and S. Whittle (Eds.), *Transgender Studies Reader* (pp. 552–564). New York, NY: Routledge.

Watson, E., & Giffney, N. (Eds.) (2017). *Clinical Encounters in Sexuality: Psychoanalytic Practice and Queer Theory.* Goleta, CA: Punctum Books.

Williams, C. (2014). Transgender. *Transgender Studies Quarterly*, *1*(1–2): 232–234.


## Question of embodiment

Cavanagh, S. L. (2018). Transgender embodiment: A Lacanian approach. *Psychoanalytic Review, 105*(3): 303–327.

Elliot, P. (2001). A psychoanalytic reading of transsexual embodiment. *Studies in Gender and Sexuality, 2*(4): 295–325.

Gozlan, O. (2008). The accident of gender. *The Psychoanalytic Review, 95*(4): 541–570.

Gozlan, O. (2016). Uncanniness at Wellesley College: The return of the transsexual. *Studies of Gender and Sexuality, 17*(4): 297–305.

Harris, A. (2008). *Gender as Soft Assembly.* New York, NY: Routledge.

Saketopoulou, A. (2014). When the body propositions gender: Reply to commentaries. *Journal of the American Psychoanalytic Assosiation, 62*(5): 823–833.

Salamon, G. (2010). *Assuming a Body: Transgender and the Rhetorics of Materiality.* New York, NY: Columbia University Press.


## Sexual difference

Cavanagh, S. L. (2016). Transsexuality as sinthome: Bracha L. Ettinger and the other (feminine) sexual difference. *Studies in Gender and Sexuality, 17*(1): 27–44.

Dimen, M. (1991). Deconstructing difference: Gender, splitting, and transitional space. *Psychoanalytic Dialogues, 1*(3): 335–352.

Fiorini, L., & Vainer, A. (2003). The sexed body and the real—its meaning in transsexualism. In: A. M. Alizade (Ed.), *Masculine Scenarios* (pp. 101–108). New York, NY: Karnac.

Gherovici, P. (2017). *Transgender Psychoanalysis: A Lacanian Perspective on Sexual Difference.* New York, NY: Routledge.

Gozlan, O. (2011). Pictogram and the myth of sexual difference. *Other/Wise.* Retrieved from https://ifpe.wordpress.com/2011/04/15/pictogram/

Gozlan, O. (2013). Transsexuality as a state of mind. *Division Review,* 7: 26–28.

Irigaray, L. (1984). *An Ethics of Sexual Difference.* New York, NY: Cornell University Press.

Lemma, A. (2013). The body one has and the body one is: Understanding the transsexual's need to be seen. *The International Journal of Psycho-Analysis, 94*(2): 277–292.

## Pedagogical dilemmas

Britzman, D. P. (2006). Little Hans, Fritz, and Ludo: On the curious history of gender in the psychoanalytic archive. *Studies in Gender and Sexuality, 7*(2): 113–140.

Gherovici, P. (2018). Psychoanalysis needs a sex change. In: O. Gozlan (Ed.), *Current Critical Debates in the Field of Transsexual Studies: In Transition* (pp. 75–88). New York, NY: Routledge.

Gozlan, O. (2017, June 27). Transsexuality as an emotional situation, aesthetics and a state of mind: A question of difference. Retrieved from https://publicseminar.org/essays/transsexuality-as-an-emotional-situation-aesthetics-and-a-state-of-mind/

Gozlan, O. (2020). Does the (fantastic) transwoman exist? A commentary on the Chilean film *A Fantastic Woman* by Sebastian Leilo and the question of psychoanalytic pedagogy. *Division/Review, A Quarterly Psychoanalytic Forum, 21,* Spring: 4–7.

## Literary and aesthetic dimensions

Amir, D. (2018). The two sleeps of Orlando: Transsexuality as caesura or cut. In: O. Gozlan (Ed.), *Current Critical Debates in the Field of Transsexual Studies: In Transition* (pp. 36–47). New York, NY: Routledge.

di Ceglie, D. (2018). The use of metaphors in understanding atypical gender identity development and its psychosocial impact. *Journal of Child Psychotherapy, 44*(1): 5–28.

Dorenbaum, D. (2018). Revisiting the friends of the Place Blanche: The transgender imaginary through the photographs of Christer Stromholm. In: O. Gozlan (Ed.), *Current Critical Debates in the Field of Transsexual Studies: In Transition* (pp. 15–35). New York, NY: Routledge.

Salah, T. (2018). To return to Schreber: Trans literature as psychoanalysis. In: O. Gozlan (Ed.), *Current Critical Debates in the Field of Transsexual Studies: In Transition* (pp. 169–180). New York, NY: Routledge.

## Memoirs/auto theory

Boylan, J. F. (2013). *Stuck in the Middle with You: A Memoir of Parenting in Three Genders*. New York, NY: Crown.

Carl, P. (2020, February 1). Becoming a man: The story of a transition. *The New York Times*. Retrieved from https://www.nytimes.com/2020/02/01/books/review/becoming-a-man-p-carl.html

Mock, J. (2017). *Surpassing Certainties: What My Twenties Taught Me*. Toronto, Canada: Simon & Schuster.

Nelson, M. (2016). *The Argonauts*. Minneapolis, MN: Graywolf Press.

## Research/clinical guides

Byne, W., Karasic, D. H., Coleman, E., Eyler, A. E., Kidd, J. D., Meyer-Bahlburg, H. F. L., Pleak, R. R., & Pula, J. (2018). Gender dysphoria in adults: An overview and primer for psychiatrists. *Transgender Health, 3*(1): 57–70.

Drescher, J. (2010). Queer diagnoses: Parallels and contrasts in the history of homosexuality, gender variance, and the *Diagnostic and Statistical Manual* (DSM). *Archives of Sexual Behavior, 39*: 427–460.

Drescher, J. (2015). Queer diagnoses revisited: The past and future of homosexuality and gender diagnoses in DSM and ICD. *International Review of Psychiatry, 27*(5): 386–395.

Drescher, J., Cohen-Kettenis, P. T., & Winter, S. (2012). Minding the body: Situating gender diagnoses in the ICD-11. *International Review of Psychiatry, 24*(6): 568–577.

Hidalgo, M. A., Ehrensaft, D., Tishelman, A. C., Clark, L. F., Garofalo, R., Rosenthal, S. M., Spack, N. P., & Olson, J. (2013, January 1). The gender affirmative model: What we know and what we aim to learn. *Human Development, 56*(5): 285–290.

Katz-Wise, S. L., Sansfaçon, A. P., Bogart, L. M., Rosal, M. C., Ehrensaft, D., Goldman, R. E., & Austin, S. B. (2019, June 1). Lessons from a community-based participatory research study with transgender and gender nonconforming youth and their families. *Action Research, 17*(2): 186–207.

Leli, U., & Drescher, J. (Eds.) (2004). *Transgender Subjectivities: A Clinician's Guide.* New York, NY: Harrington Park.

Olson-Kennedy, J., Chan, Y. M., Rosenthal, S., Hidalgo, M. A., Chen, D., Clark L., Ehrensaft, D., Tishelman, A., & Garofalo, R. (2019). Creating the trans youth research network: A collaborative research endeavor. *Transgender Health, 4*(1): 304–312.

Stein, A. (2018). *Unbound: Transgender Men and the Remaking of Identity.* New York, NY: Pantheon.

Winter, S., Ehrensaft, D., Telfer, M., T'Sjoen, G., Koh, J., Pickstone-Taylor, S., Kruger, A., Griffin, L., Foigel, M., De Cuypere, G., & Karasic, D. (2019). ICD-11 and gender incongruence of childhood: A rethink is needed. *The Lancet: Child and Adolescent Health, 3*(10): 671–673.

## Ethical dilemmas/controversies

Chen, D., Stancin, T., Edward-Leeper, L., & Tishelman, A. (2018). Advancing the practice of pediatric psychology with transgender youth: State of the science, ongoing controversies, and future directions. *Clinical Practice in Pediatric Psychology, 6*(1): 73–83.

Drescher, J., Cohen-Kettenis, P. T., & Reed, G. M. (2016). Gender incongruence of childhood in the ICD-11: Controversies, proposals and rational. *Lancet Psychiatry, 3*: 297–304.

Drescher, J., & Pula, J. (2014). Ethical issues raised by the treatment of gender variant prepubescent children. *The Hastings Center Report, 44*(Suppl 4): S17–22.

Ehrensaft, D. (2012). From gender identity disorder to gender identity creativity: True gender self child therapy. *Journal of Homosexuality, 59*(3): 337–356.

Gozlan, O. (2018). From continuity to contiguity: A response to the fraught temporality of gender. *Psychoanalytic Review, 105*(1): 1–29.

Steensma, T. D., & Cohen-Kettenis, P. T. (2018). A critical commentary on follow-up studies and "desistence" theories about transgender and gender non-conforming children. *International Journal of Transgenderism, 19*(1): 225–230.

Temple Newhook, J., Payne, J., Winters, K., Feder, S., Holmes, C., Tosh, J., Sinnott, M. L., Jaimieson, A., & Pickett, S. (2018). A critical commentary on follow-up studies and "desistance" theories about transgender and gender-nonconforming children. *International Journal of Transgenderism, 19*(2): 212–224.

Turban, J. L., & Ehrensaft, D. (2018). Research review: Gender identity in youth—Treatment paradigms and controversies. *Journal of Child Psychology and Psychiatry, and Allied Disciplines, 59*(12): 1228–1243.

Zucker, K. J. (2018). The myth of persistence: Response to "A critical commentary on follow-up studies and 'desistance' theories about transgender and gender non-conforming children" by Temple Newhook et al. *International Journal of Transgenderism, 19*(1): 231–245.

# CHAPTER NINE

# Gay women and the Boston Psychoanalytic Society and Institute

*Shari Thurer*

> *Remember the ladies ...*
>
> —Abigail Adams

There is a glaring omission in most theorizing about homosexuality: lesbianism (by which I, of course, do not mean a phylum of illness, but a slippery point on the sexual-orientation continuum). In 1998, a research team calculated that the entire psychoanalytic literature on female homosexuality reported on fewer than a hundred individuals. This lack of psychoanalytic consideration probably mirrors the marginalization of lesbians at large, where women suffer the double ignominy of being both female and homosexual. Lesbianism is paradoxically everywhere and nowhere, for it remains unnoticed when it is in plain sight. Psychoanalyst Anton Kris, a highly respected and recently deceased BPSI elder statesman, reported that until recently, male homosexuality was "anathema," while female homosexuality was "overlooked." Lesbianism is conspicuous by its absence even in the early work of second-wave feminist analysts like Juliet Mitchell and Jessica Benjamin. Female homosexuals are only recently finding their voice; among the very few is Susan Vaughan of New York, who writes movingly about lesbian parenting (Vaughan, personal communication).

This voicelessness seems to be true in Boston, where the lesbian analysts and candidates I contacted—and there are very few— were reluctant to speak with me. Indeed, they are very busy, but it is interesting to contrast their response with that of the male homosexuals, who were eager to talk about their experience at BPSI. The numbers are so small that it would be unfair to draw any conclusions about their reticence. I did glean a few thoughts from these women on the matter: one individual argued that psychoanalytic theory (as taught at the Boston Psychoanalytic Society and Institute) is homophobic in that it equates mental health with the heterosexual marriage bed. She also believed that developmental theory (as conveyed by the Institute) cannot account for positive, healthy homosexuality—for which there is no paradigm. On the other hand, Paola Contreras, a sixth-year candidate (at the time), who is lesbian, felt that she has been listened to and heard in her training, which, she pointed out, encouraged critical thinking. She perceived herself to be strongly supported by faculty and supervisors (personal communication).

Diane O'Donoghue, an affiliate scholar member who has been the co-instructor of the "Gender and Sexuality" seminar that is now required of fourth-year candidates, was a lesbian member of the BPSI Task Force on LGBTQ issues through its two decades of existence. She would characterize the challenges for BPSI as both acknowledging and redressing the past, and making an institutional commitment to advancing progressive contemporary practices, both clinically and critically, in our work with patients and colleagues, and in our relevant scholarly pursuits. She notes that resistances to an intrapsychic and heteronormative construction of "sex," foundational at the origins of psychoanalytic thinking, often looked to relational and attachment models that, unwittingly, could diminish the importance of the dynamic and vital role of "sexualities" (personal communication). The return to the BPSI curriculum of a class that addresses these issues in current clinical and academic literature marks an important acknowledgment of the need to again, in a very different way, foreground this as a decisive topic. It can be argued that the vibrancy of current published work involving LGBTQ patients and/or clinicians, a crucial component of this class, also has relevance within broader contemporary discourse, where it rightly deserves a place of influence.

Clearly, I was encountering the "Rashoman effect," in which different women gave me subjective, and sometimes contradictory, accounts of their experience at BPSI. To be sure, there are probably as many BPSI analyst and therapist attitudes toward homosexuality and gender as there are BPSI analysts and therapists. If there is to be progress toward a unified, sensible theory about sexuality and gender, we should capitalize on the broad-based intellectual ferment and develop paradigms that are unbiased, fact-based, and useful to a "rainbow" of sexual behaviors, identities, and feelings. I applaud the APsaA's recent *mea culpa* regarding their past homophobia, and BPSI following suit. I suggest that continued theoretical humility be in order. Therapists should maintain an actively skeptical stance as they proceed with their clinical work. After all, the most compelling stories unfold when you don't start out with the answer. Modestly, collectively, we may, to quote Alexander Portnoy's psychoanalyst, "perhaps to begin."

# Index